The Sky's the Limit

How to Experience the True Abundant Life

Del Edwards

Belleville, Ontario, Canada

The Sky's the Limit
Copyright © 2003, Del Edwards

All Scripture quotations, unless otherwise specified, are from *The Holy Bible, King James Version.* Copyright © 1977, 1984, Thomas Nelson Inc., Publishers.

Cover design by Lorna Hylton

ISBN: 1-55306-611-1
LSI Edition: 1-55306-613-8

**For more information or
to order additional copies, please contact:**
Del Edwards
P.O. Box 51033, Unit 379
25 Peel Centre Dr.
Brampton, ON Canada
L6T 5M2

Guardian Books is an imprint of *Essence Publishing,* a Christian Book Publisher dedicated to furthering the work of Christ through the written word. For more information, contact:
20 Hanna Court, Belleville, Ontario, Canada K8P 5J2
Phone: 1-800-238-6376 • Fax: (613) 962-3055
E-mail: publishing@essencegroup.com
Internet: www.essencegroup.com

Dedication

This book is dedicated to Jesus Christ the Righteous King. If it were not for His sacrifice on Calvary, there would be no book; there would be nothing to tell of His wondrous love toward us, of His divine process in bringing us through to healing. We thank God for the ministry He has entrusted to us.

This book is also dedicated to the persons featured within it, who have opened their lives so that others might be healed. They had the courage to be honest about what really happens in the heart of a Christian and how there is an answer for those fleshly failures—deliverance through the Blood of Jesus Christ. Finally, this book is dedicated to you, the reader. May you find answers, in these pages, for which you have been searching. May He lead you into the reality of His Spirit, in His ability to expose a heart to nakedness and clothe it in His righteousness. May you understand what you read and may you endeavour to allow the Lord Jesus entrance into the deep recesses that He sees and desires to change.

May this book be used to change many lives for the glory of His precious Name.

Prologue

I had a dream that we were having a book review. I stood up to pray, but there was confusion—people were talking. I stood up to pray again, because people kept on talking. Then, I spoke forth all that God would accomplish for the glory of His Name through this book. Still these people were not serious. I also spoke that God had given me direction for this book, and that we would go to a second book or a series of books. I shared, as well, how this book came about, that we were walking one morning after a Trinidad missionary trip, and the Scriptures God gave me in Jeremiah (Jer. 50:2).

So, obviously, God wanted us to move ahead with this book. We don't know what God has in store, but it is God's book. The true vision behind this book is the need to write about our lives, so that people can understand and that they can be healed. *"The Lord gave the word: great was the company of those that published it"* (Psalm 68:11).

Declare ye among the nations, and publish, and set up a standard; publish, and conceal not: say, Babylon is taken, Bel is confounded, Merodach is broken in pieces; her idols are confounded, her images are broken in pieces (Jeremiah 50:2).

That I may publish with the voice of thanksgiving, and tell of all thy wondrous works (Psalm 26:7).

I will stand upon my watch, and set me upon the tower, and will watch to see what he will say unto me, and what I shall answer when I am reproved. And the Lord answered me, and said, Write the vision, and make it plain upon tables, that he may run that readeth it. For the vision is yet for an appointed time, but at the end it shall speak, and not lie: though it tarry, wait for it; because it will surely come, it will not tarry (Habakkuk 2:1–3).

Moreover the Lord said unto me, Take thee a great roll, and write in it with a man's pen concerning Mahershalalhashbaz. And I took unto me faithful witnesses to record, Uriah the priest, and Zechariah the son of Jeberechiah (Isaiah 8:1–2).

The Lord has given us the Word, the vision and the people—so we have moved forward. The testimonies are real and the events described factual, as lived through the lives of those who allowed the Lord to expose them with such love and gentleness. The pure intention behind this book is to illustrate the truth about one's past and how God can restore a soul—even yours.

You will notice that those who have opened up their lives have not disclosed their names; nor are the names of those mentioned in the testimonies disclosed. This is not out of an intention to deceive or because there is any shame associated with these testimonies. They are not meant to bring shame to the individuals that played a role in the formation of these characters or to shame families that did the best they could with what they had. The families and those mentioned in these testimonies are still living, and some have never heard their lives shared with such depth. So, anonymity is to respect the privacy of family and friends around the individuals featured in this book.

Of more importance than these testimonies are the messages ministered over the years that have brought these lives forth. The messages selected for this book have probably been ones with the most impact and will provide great blessings to the reader with an open heart. To help the reader understand the essence of what God spoke, the messages have been abridged. We encourage you to contact the ministry for teaching tapes and to search out the Scriptures for yourself, in the light that the Word was brought forth. May this book open new dimensions in your understanding of the Word of God.

A Brief Background

My father, Randolph Linton—known to most as Brother Rannie—was born on April 1, 1904. At the tender age of twelve, he was met with a divine visitation. The heavens opened, and an angel whose form reached up unto the sky touched his hands and anointed him with all nine gifts of the Spirit. It was all he could do to run home and yell to his mom, "Mama, Mama, God has come, God has come!" So was the beginning of a work still ongoing today.

My father had a tremendous ministry and flowed in all of the nine gifts of the Spirit. I was raised in the church. My father and mother were both very gentle and loving with all of their children, and admonished and trained us in the ways of the Lord. Both of my parents are enjoying the presence of their Saviour, as they have both died and now see Him face to face.

I have been a Christian for most of my life and I thank God for my heritage. I married Neville Edwards, a very loving man with whom I share a ministry as pastors of Mount

Zion House of Praise. We also lead mission teams and travel to different lands several times a year.

My prayer is that this book blesses you, and that the messages imparted to me over the years by the Lord Jesus will be used to heal your body, soul and spirit. To Him be all praise and honour and glory.

Message from My Daughter, Lorna Hylton

This message was written on behalf of all three of my children—Richard, Lorna, and Julie—by my daughter Lorna.

First of all, thank you, Mom, for giving me this opportunity to be a part of this great book that God has prompted you to write—what an honour. I know that I speak for Richard and Julie as I write this. This is a tribute to a selfless woman; a woman who puts God first in everything—my mother.

If someone were to ask me what kind of woman I desire to become, I would say, "Like my mom." She is a woman of wisdom and grace. She represents beauty, virtue and strength. The beauty of Christ within her fills her being and flows out onto those she touches.

She has touched the hearts of thousands worldwide; from Europe to Africa to the Caribbean, North, Central and South America. She is God's servant, in the true sense of the word. She serves God's people every day of her life, unselfishly, and she loves without condition. She truly loves the Body of Christ.

Her words from the Holy Spirit have incredible power that have challenged and changed many. Her words have built me up emotionally over my lifetime, giving me a confidence in myself that will never dissipate. Her love is sustained and deep. Whenever I felt overwhelmed by Satan's attack, there she would be with a prayer, a soft word or simply a healing embrace that would empower me. People are drawn to her because of the strength of God's love within her. She tells it like it is, without "beating around the bush." She knows just what to say. It's by God's grace and wisdom that she has been a help to thousands.

My mother raised me and then freed me to walk on my own, leaving me in God's hands. She always taught me to stand strong and confident in God, because Satan wants to defeat you, but you cannot let him. Anything is possible, as long as we put God first and trust Him in all things. There is a tie so strong between my mother and I, that nothing can break it. I call it "the unbreakable bond."

If only I could repay her with as much love and respect as she has shown me. I will not attain unto that, but I can pray that God will keep her strong and continuously provide for all her needs. I can pray that God richly blesses her and endows her with more of His wisdom, as she continues to strive for perfection.

God gave my mother that rarest gift; an understanding heart, a gentle, kindly manner and wisdom to impart. She has built character in many as a lasting tribute to Jesus Christ. The lives she has touched, the good she does, shall never know an end. I am proud to call her mother; my confidante, my friend.

Thank you, Mom, for everything, but most of all for teaching me and nurturing me according to God's laws. I love you and appreciate you, so much.

—*Lorna*

> *She looketh well to the ways of her household, and eateth not the bread of idleness. Her children arise up, and call her blessed; her husband also, and he praiseth her. Many daughters have done virtuously, but thou excellest them all. Favour is deceitful, and beauty is vain: but a woman that feareth the Lord, she shall be praised. Give her of the fruit of her hands; and let her own works praise her in the gates* (Proverbs 31:27–31).

Chapter 1

The Green Berets

God has called my husband and I into a ministry that is not easy. The fivefold ministry of pastors, teachers, apostles, prophets and evangelists (Ephesians 4:11) is to perfect the saints for the work of the ministry. This work of perfecting the saints has meant for us to be willing to correct those whom God has given us to work with and to train them in the ministry.

As you will read in the testimonies interspersed throughout this book, the process of training and correction is not easy. Many times I have had to stand on what God had shown me about someone's heart, until He opened that person's eyes. Many pastors and leaders tend to shy away from the true work of correction and perfection with God's people—sometimes for fear of diminishing their numbers. And not everyone in the Body of Christ, particularly those who have been wounded, is willing to submit to the authority and correction of a pastor.

But my husband and I have always focused on Jesus Christ, and we want all that He has for His people. We will not settle for anything less for ourselves or for His people. While Christians may not fully understand the ministry of correction motivated only by love, the Lord knows them that are His, and they will not faint when they are reproved of Him.

Therefore, while we were travelling in Trinidad, a pastor observed that our ministry is not for everyone. How true his statement was when he likened our ministry to the hard training and discipline necessary for members of the "Green Berets." He also mentioned that not everyone would be willing to undergo this training in order to come forth. After returning from that trip, I felt a sadness in my spirit because of different issues we had to deal with between team members. I could not remember ever feeling such distress. Then I had a dream.

I dreamt that we were on a missionary trip, going from one place to another. We encountered a wall around which there seemed to be absolutely no way; we were at a standstill. I looked up at the wall and I saw that there was a ridge. Then I realized that I could climb up on this ridge. I do not know how I got up over that wall, but I leaped over and got to the other side.

So, I knew that God had spoken a message deep in my spirit. The first Scripture that came to my heart was 2 Samuel 22:30—*"by my God have I leaped over a wall."* Despite the fact that we were fighting demonic oppression while in Trinidad, the Lord really encouraged me through the dream and this message. I started by reading all of 2 Samuel 22.

For thou art my lamp, O Lord: and the Lord will lighten my darkness. For by thee I have run through a troop: by my God have I leaped over a wall. As for God, his way is perfect; the word of the Lord is tried: he is a buckler to all them that trust in him (2 Samuel 22:29–31).

As I read through the chapter, I realized that this was not only for David, but for the Church as well. And I was very encouraged. I realized that if we are walking with God in the realm of the Spirit, we are unconquerable. No devil can conquer God's people. I am not saying that Satan will fail to put up a fight, but thank You, Jesus, God is real! He does and will fight for us! Then, I studied several Scriptures on running through a troop, including this one:

There shall no man be able to stand before you: for the Lord your God shall lay the fear of you and the dread of you upon all the land that ye shall tread upon, as he hath said unto you (Deuteronomy 11:25).

Other references are found in Deuteronomy 28:7; Joshua 1:5–9; Joshua 21:44; Joshua 23:9 and Isaiah 33:16. Another point in the dream was that only one person made it over the wall. Some people in the dream were following me, and I told them to go back and to take another path, because I knew they were not going to be able to make the climb. I was led to the conclusion that it takes strength to climb that mountaintop. This walk of holiness and discipline is not for the weak and fearful, nor for the sinful. So, I studied the word "strength."

In that day shall the Lord of hosts be for a crown of glory, and for a diadem of beauty, unto the residue of his people, And for a spirit of judgment to him that sitteth in judgment, and for strength to them that turn the battle to the gate (Isaiah 28:5–6).

But they that wait upon the Lord shall renew their strength; they shall mount up with wings as eagles; they shall run, and not be weary; and they shall walk, and not faint (Isaiah 40:31).

Other references can be found in 2 Samuel 22:40; Daniel 11:32 and Ephesians 3:16. These Scriptures point to the fact that we have to be strengthened to fight the enemy. And God has given us enough of His Word to know that the end of the age is here. We are going to face challenges we have never before had to face. Are we going to fall at these trials? No, the Lord has given us His Word, and with Him, we can make it.

But God hath chosen the foolish things of the world to confound the wise; and God hath chosen the weak things of the world to confound the things which are mighty (1 Corinthians 1:27. Read also Colossians 1:11 and Psalm 8:2).

This is God's supernatural strength and this is what He has given us. God's strength goes past what human flesh can do.

In that dream, it was impossible for me to climb the wall; I knew in my heart that only God could carry me over. And I know that we are going to come up against serious attacks—this is a serious hour about which the Church has been warned many times. It is time that the Church realize that Satan wants to destroy our lives. One of the ways he does this is by using our minds, hearts and souls to sin against God. He uses us as tools in his hands to bring division and confusion to the Body of Christ. Many times, when a test comes to prove us, we fail to understand the Word of God as He intended us to and we fall in sin.

Rather, we should stand firm and challenge the enemy, saying: "God has given me power and I will **not** sin!" Too often we allow the enemy to rob us, to move us away from our steadfastness, and we open up our hearts to demonic forces. No matter how Satan tries to attack me, I am determined that, through the power of Jesus' name, he is not going to win.

God has given us His Word, His Name, His Spirit and His Blood. He has given us everything we need. We are equipped from top to bottom, yet we allow the devil to take advantage of us. God is going to keep us in these times. With that determination, it does not matter what the enemy tries; we are going to stand and glorify the love of God. It is time to love Jesus.

And he said unto me, My grace is sufficient for thee: for my strength is made perfect in weakness. Most gladly therefore will I rather glory in my infirmities, that the power of Christ may rest upon me. Therefore I take pleasure in infirmities, in reproaches, in necessities, in persecutions, in distresses for Christ's sake: for when I am weak, then am I strong (2 Corinthians 12:9–10. Read also 2 Corinthians 13:4 and Hebrews 11:33–34).

This led me to research Scriptures on "God, our strength." Only through Him can we conquer. It is time we knew that in our hearts in a practical way. It is time that we faced Satan and refused to turn our backs on God through sin.

"*Blessed is the man whose strength is in thee; in whose heart are the ways of them*" (Psalm 84:5). Other references to "God, our strength" can be found in Exodus 15:2; Psalm 18:1; Psalm 28:8; Psalm 46:1; Psalm 73:26; Psalm 81:1; Psalm 89:21 and 2 Samuel 22:30.

He is a God who can see us through any affliction and trial, without falling into sin. David could have turned his back on God because of all that he went through, but he knew his God would preserve him. David said that it was through his God that he leaped over a wall. In saying that, he was acknowledging a victorious God. And we know that, though our walls seem higher and more impossible than others', God is going to give us that type of strength. He is the only One who can. Whatever wall you face—the wall of sickness, the wall of financial hardship or the wall of pain—whatever your wall might be, God is going to allow you to climb over it.

Too often, however, we forget His Word and we resort back to the flesh. There is a lack in our hearts, and that lack leads us to sin over and over again. It is the mountain of sin in our lives that God wants us to overcome. Does it take great faith to conquer it?

No, because His Word tells us that a mustard seed of faith can tell that mountain to be removed! We have that faith in us now and we must exercise it. God is able to do all things through our lives. Remember: the hard training of a "Green Beret," disciplined and chastened to walk a holy life, is for the whosoever. But unfortunately, not everyone is willing to submit to His full authority over our lives.

I believe the Lord is saying that we are going to face more challenges and we had better be ready to face them victoriously, and work above sin. Wickedness is going to escalate and God is going to put us to the test to bring us forth as gold. Gold is the pure divinity of His Kingdom and His full authority over our lives. By His grace it is possible to walk through each and every test and trial with unyielding determination not to sin.

This is an abridged version of this message.
Please contact us to order the tape of
this entire message.

Chapter 2

The Church Is in Darkness

One morning, I woke up and heard the word "darkness." I then realized God was not speaking to me about the world, but rather about the Church. It is the Church that is in darkness. And one of the reasons why the Church is in darkness is that we have not studied the Word of God. It is good that the fivefold (apostles, prophets, teachers, evangelists and pastors) ministries are in the Body of Christ to minister His Word, but we have to know and search the Scriptures for ourselves.

The study of the Word, or even listening to messages, is not about head knowledge. A true student of the Word is one who is a doer, not a hearer only. I have travelled to many different lands and have visited countless churches, and when I survey the church on the whole, we are weaklings and are quickly dislocated. We are quickly malicious. We are quickly angered and slow to forgive. We have no love. The world is looking for a true manifestation of sons of God. When Jesus returns, it will be to glorify Himself in a Church that has no spot or wrinkle. He died to raise up sons, walking in His image and likeness, and we must examine our hearts. We must understand what it is in our hearts that hinders us from walking in the realm of the Spirit. He who has ears to hear, let him hear.

Today, there is definitely a famine of hearing the Word of God, as Amos prophesied:

> *Behold, the days come, saith the Lord God, that I will send a famine in the land, not a famine of bread, nor a thirst for water, but of hearing the words of the Lord: And they shall wander from sea to sea, and from the north even to the east, they shall run to and fro to seek the word of the Lord, and shall not find it* (Amos 8:11–12).

We know this to be true because we see Christians remaining unchanged, going to church Sunday after Sunday. And yet, Christ has told us to put off the old man and to put on the Lord Jesus Christ. So, how is the Lord going to do it?

Satan will not give up easily, so we have got to press in and take Jesus at His Word. We have to spend time in prayer. We have to spend time in praise and worship to our God. We have to spend time with the Body of Christ. We need one another. As I turned to the Scriptures, it became clearer.

> *But we have this treasure in earthen vessels, that the excellency of the power may be of God, and not of us* (2 Corinthians 4:7. Read also 2 Corinthians 4:6–11).

To a large extent, the Church has not understood His Word. Many do not believe that Jesus can be fully made manifest in our flesh and that we can walk above sin. God is able to demolish the darkness in us. He demolished the darkness when the earth was a void without form. When there was nothing, He created life. He wants to create His life in us following the same pattern. That's the purpose of Jesus Christ in us; there is a lot of darkness in this world, and the Christian has to shine so the world will see Jesus.

He didn't say it was going to be easy, but He did promise us His glory. He promised us joy, peace and righteousness in the Holy Ghost. He promised us the fruit of the Spirit. And no man can take that away from us. He wants to rid us of our darkness, so that the glorious light of the gospel can shine out of our hearts and radiate through our lives.

> We have also a more sure word of prophecy; whereunto ye do well that ye take heed, as unto a light that shineth in a dark place, until the day dawn, and the day star arise in your hearts (2 Peter 1:19. Read also Genesis 1:1–3; Psalm 119:105 and John 5:35–47).

The church is often seasonal, hot and cold. Jesus is greater than all and has come to give us light, yet we remain in darkness. The Word of God testifies of Him. Yet, all too often, Christians struggle with a message about cleansing their hearts. Preach about how to be happy, and we run out of the church happy. But when we go home, we behave so sinfully. We gossip, yell at our families and have unforgiveness in our hearts. We should be open books. What we are in church is what we must be out in the world. I am not saying it is easy—we have to die to self daily.

Although Jesus Christ was the Son of God, the religious elite of His day did not believe Him. The devil has wreaked havoc with God's people and we do not know what to believe. If it feels good, we believe it. The realm of the Spirit is not by feeling! We have to know the Word of God. There is a lack in the Church which we must address, because it is only going to become more difficult to walk as a Christian. What kind of fruit are we producing? Our fruit should be the fruit of the Spirit referred to by the Scriptures.

The light of the glory of God is in us, but often we look for external experiences. I used to want a thunderbolt from heaven to change me instantly. I soon learned that I had to drop on my knees and cry out to God. I learned that I had to fast and seek God. I learned that I had to present my heart daily before God and let Him cleanse me with His Blood. I learned that I had to go through the process of deliverance. For example, one of my dark areas was anger. I was a very angry person. God had to put a searchlight on my heart and deliver me from that anger. When I understood that God's new covenant grace does not "cover" sin, but remits it, I knew that I could walk in freedom from sin. How, when we are so cluttered with sin, may the light of Jesus shine through us? We need to be effective Christians today and He died to set us free.

The mind is the battleground for the enemy. That's where most of our darkness lies. The devil programs us with his wickedness. But we should be at the place to deliver the Church from problems with which the enemy has oppressed us. We, as the children of God, have the power to gird up our mind and to bring it back into subjection. My mind is going to be the Christ-mind. He will not let the devil take advantage of us, if we take hold of His Word.

Church, we can do great exploits for God. We can take this world. If twelve disciples took Jerusalem in their day, and turned it upside down, then what has happened to the Church today? God is the same God who can take us out of darkness. It is time for us to rise up and take what the Word of God says and know that it is real. We believe any voice out there instead of the Word of God. I am determined, however, to destroy Satan's kingdom in my life.

> *Who are kept by the power of God through faith unto salvation ready to be revealed in the last time* (1 Peter 1:5—read 1 Peter 1:1–14).

One of the most prominent sins of the Church today is disobedience. This is one of the reasons why the children of Israel did not come into the Promised Land. Sometimes, when I observe Christians' behaviour, I have to wonder what Bible we are reading, because the Word of God is not changing us at all. Jesus knows our problems and came to purify us so that we could stand the greater trials ahead. There is a soulish part of us where evil spirits lodge, but Jesus died to restore our souls as He did with the apostle Paul:

> *And I said, Who art thou, Lord? And he said, I am Jesus whom thou persecutest. But rise, and stand upon thy feet: for I have appeared unto thee for this purpose, to make thee a minister and a witness both of these things which thou hast seen, and of those things in the which I will appear*

unto thee (Acts 26:15–16. Read also Acts 26:17–18 and John 1:1–5).

In the beginning was the Word. God, who spoke in Genesis, was there from the beginning, and was the same Jesus. We cannot exist with light unless it is Jesus' light in us. The works of Jesus Christ have to be manifested in us. The Word of Jesus Christ has to be completed in us. Darkness cannot comprehend this. As Jesus said, because our deeds are evil, we are often not willing to come to that light.

> *Then spake Jesus again unto them, saying, I am the light of the world: he that followeth me shall not walk in darkness, but shall have the light of life* (John 8:12. Read also John 8:35–36, 44–47 and 51).

Church, we have to change. We have to be lights in dark places. If we are fulfilling the lusts of the flesh, we are working after our father, the devil. And we seem to believe his lies more than we believe God. But he *is* a liar—he was a liar from the beginning and he will lie to us.

We need to start praising God. When we feel pain, we should start to praise God. Why don't we believe the report of the Word of God? Why do we believe the report of the devil? Church, we need to love the Word. There was a time when I read the Bible ritualistically and I got very little out of it. I feel that we do not fully understand that the Word is life giving. We must ask the Lord to reveal Himself to us through His Word.

> *Wherefore he saith, Awake thou that sleepest, and arise from the dead, and Christ shall give thee light* (Ephesians 5:14— read Ephesians 5:14–21).

I believe if there is any time we need to awaken, it is now. He wants to put the cross to our lives so that He can give us life. This means that we should not give life to the sin warring in our bodies. We need to arise with this Word. He is sovereign and He knows what we are going through. Those who lay down their lives will find it in Him. This is the light of His resurrection.

> *And the city had no need of the sun, neither of the moon, to shine in it: for the glory of God did lighten it, and the Lamb is the light thereof* (Revelation 21:23).

What a place to be at, where the devil comes and finds nothing in us. Our lives must point people to Jesus. Old Testament saints used the blood of goats and bulls, but Jesus Christ came to cleanse us, to remit our sins and take them away, with His own Blood. This means we should not keep sinning before Him—when we continue to do the same sins over and over, we are saying that His Blood has no effect.

James 5:16a directs believers to confess their faults one to another, and pray one for another that they might be healed. To get rid of our darkness, and for God to set us free, we need to find in the Body of Christ someone we can confide in. We cannot do it in our own strength. We need the Word of God, the Blood of Jesus and the Body of Christ.

This is why God has created a body, so that we can pray one for another. God is going to have a people who are pure; He is going to have a people who are holy and who shine His light. Our righteousness is as filthy rags. It is time we move into the righteousness of the Lord. God is going to judge His people. God will destroy flesh. God is not interested in our money—He is interested in our obedience. He is not interested in the external—He is interested in the internal heart. He wants to cleanse our souls.

> *Therefore night shall be unto you, that ye shall not have a vision; and it shall be dark unto you, that ye shall not divine; and the sun shall go down over the prophets, and the day shall be dark over them"* (Micah 3:6. See other references, Micah 3:1–5, 7–12; Matthew 6:21–34 and John 3:19–21).

Sometimes we are inclined to think that Christians have no darkness. And yet we see that backbiting, envy, division and strife are commonplace in the church. This is darkness, and it covers up the light.

God knows our hearts. Our lives should be an open book. We should not be afraid of our hearts. God wants us to get rid of the darkness and stop covering it up. When we cover up, Satan eventually leads us to backslide, but when we open our hearts, Jesus sets us free to continue walking in the light with Him. We have to bring our darkness to the light, whatever it might be. There is no reason why we should sin before God when He has made provision. He is gracious, merciful, loving, tender and kind. He is everything that we need. He has made provision for us to change. He will not lower His standard, established in His Word. We cannot say that we have light and continue in sin. *"Ye are all the children of light, and the children of the day: we are not of the night, nor of darkness"* (1 Thessalonians 5:5).Other references can be found in John 13:11–14; Galatians 5:15–17 and 1 Thessalonians 5:1–4, 6–8.

Our flesh wants to take pre-eminence; it wants to be seen. Once we accept Jesus, however, light is already in us to expel the darkness and deaden the flesh. We often make the mistake of thinking that His work of righteousness is complete when we pray the sinner's prayer at salvation, but we must deal with our hearts so we can measure up to the Word. His Word is a mirror, in which our lives should be reflected.

> *But if we walk in the light, as he is in the light, we have fellowship one with another, and the blood of Jesus Christ his Son cleanseth us from all sin* (1 John 1:7.Other references, Matthew 13:13–14 and 1 John 1–6, 8–10).

These saints had the fellowship of the Father. We must fellowship around His table, around His Word. That Word must be rooted in us before we can give life. When we feel love and warmth from our brethren, it is because they have fellowship with Him. Yet there are others who are afraid to draw near to Him because of darkness. We have to present that darkness to the light in order for the light to truly heal us.

> *He that saith he is in the light, and hateth his brother, is in darkness even until now. He that loveth his brother abideth in the light, and there is none occasion of stumbling in him* (1 John 2:9–10. Read also 1 John 2:1–8, 11–13 and Ephesians 4:11–32).

We have to live this Word. Some of us need to repent of the hate that we carry inside. When we walk around with hate and bitterness, it brings all sorts of disease. Yet we still walk in darkness.

There is absolutely no reason why the Church should be ignorant, because the Holy Spirit dwells in us. It is important to know that is why God has written His Word, so that we could understand how to walk. The Church tends to get caught up in the realm of the flesh, and if we are not feeling goosebumps, we think "That's not God." Let us be sober, because God wants to speak to us through His Word.

We have to get rid of our fleshly feelings, because we are going to lose out if we don't. What is it going to take to wake us up? We need to get angry at Satan for what he has done to our children, our youth, our homes and our society. Many times we are not moved by worldly wickedness because we don't have a righteous soul to vex!

We discount what the Word of God says. Church, it is time we get back to the Word and the principles contained in the Bible. There is no reason why we should be walking in darkness. The light of Jesus Christ is in us to clear it away. If we read the Word with understanding given by the Holy Spirit, we will not walk in darkness; we will not be ignorant.

> *Woe unto them that call evil good, and good evil; that put darkness for light, and light for darkness; that put bitter for sweet, and sweet for bitter!* (Isaiah 5:20—read Isaiah 5:1–30).

Wickedness is increasing, and so must holiness increase. We must come with repentance to the Lord before we present any need. What are we doing to bring in the light? If the light doesn't come from us, then how great is the darkness in the world. He wants that light to come forth from our lives now, in this wicked darkness. If we want true fellowship and communion with the Father, we must walk in His light. It is time for us to take a stand against sin and live worthy of the light of His Great Name.

This is an abridged version of this message.
Please contact us to order the tape of
this entire message.

Chapter 3

Be Strong in the Lord

The Lord spoke this message to me at the end of 1997, for 1998: "Prepare for war." He led me into a great truth about being strong in the Lord. When the Lord says "Be strong," this usually means there are circumstances ahead that may weaken us. But His Word is real and gives us strength for the trials ahead. *"Finally, my brethren, be strong in the Lord, and in the power of his might"* (Ephesians 6:10).

The battle that we are fighting is not a fleshly battle. We are at war, but His Word guarantees victory. The victory is won when we cease fighting in the flesh and learn to praise our God, no matter what we are going through. In Isaiah 54:17, He says that no weapon formed against us will prosper, so He is warning us that weapons are going to come against us, but we must allow Him to fight our battles. When Jesus came to Pilate in the judgment hall and false accusations were brought against Him, He never opened His mouth.

The darts of the enemy are going to come from every angle. Our greatest battles will lead to our greatest victories.

God is maturing His church to a place where we will not be moved. And He matures the Church by allowing things to happen to us. We must learn to let God fight our battles, and in due season, He will bring us through. When God is fighting for us, who can be against us?

> *Be strong and courageous, be not afraid nor dismayed for the king of Assyria, nor for all the multitude that is with him: for there be more with us than with him: With him is an arm of flesh; but with us is the Lord our God to help us, and to fight our battles. And the people rested themselves upon the words of Hezekiah king of Judah* (2 Chronicles 32:7–8).

The Lord spoke to my heart: "When I say be strong, then that means prepare for war." This is the key, Church. So often we become overwhelmed with problems. There is nothing to be afraid of when God fights our battles, so prepare for war. Moses said to the children of Israel to be strong, because there was going to be warfare, but God was going to fight their battles.

> *And the Lord, he it is that doth go before thee; he will be with thee, he will not fail thee, neither forsake thee: fear not, neither be dismayed* (Deuteronomy 31:8. Read also Deuteronomy 31:1–8 and 2 Chronicles 20:15–24).

You see, once we are afraid, we have lost the battle. Satan has won. We must be delivered from that spirit of fear. If you have fear, you cannot conquer. Fear brings torment. If we look at certain situations with our natural eyes, there is going to be cause for fear; however, the battle is already won. All we have to do is stand up and see the devil run from us. Satan knows there is power in fear. As a child, I used to be fearful. But, the only fear we need today is a reverential fear of God.

And he answered, Fear not: for they that be with us are more than they that be with them. And Elisha prayed, and said, Lord, I pray thee, open his eyes, that he may see. And the Lord opened the eyes of the young man; and he saw: and, behold, the mountain was full of horses and chariots of fire round about Elisha. (2 Kings 6:16–17—read 2 Kings 6:1–33).

God is telling us not to fear because He is going to fight our battles. Everything coming was planned by God, and He knows exactly the time and the season. I believe that we are going to see the spirit and power of Elijah coming to the Church. God has invested Himself in us; we need to believe that God is speaking and to believe His Word.

"What shall we then say to these things? If God be for us, who can be against us?" (Romans 8:31. Read also Jeremiah 17:5–10; 1 John 4:4–21; Deuteronomy 8:2; Joshua 10:25, 42–43; 1 Chronicles 22:13 and 28:20). It is easy to say that we will be strong and courageous, but in some situations it is not as easy to remember the Word that God spoke to us. We must be strong in the Lord, and not in our own strength. Abide in Him—if His Word abides in us, we shall ask what we will and it shall be done. When the battle becomes hot, remember that other brothers and sisters are going through the same battles.

Don't be afraid of demonic forces. God is telling us to prepare for war. We will see and hear big things we never dreamt were possible, but our strength is in the Lord!

This is an abridged version of this message. Please contact us to order the tape of this entire message.

Chapter 4

Repentance Before Restoration or Revival

The Lord spoke to me some time ago that only when we experience true and life-changing repentance will the Church experience true restoration and revival. It is not the world that needs to repent so much—it's the Church! God is interested in our hearts, and He wants us to come to that place where the enemy finds nothing in us. It is possible to walk in that realm, but only as we are honest with our hearts and we repent before a Holy God. These thoughts led me to several Scriptures.

> *Therefore also now, saith the Lord, turn ye even to me with all your heart, and with fasting, and with weeping, and with mourning: And rend your heart, and not your garments, and turn unto the Lord your God: for he is gracious and merciful, slow to anger, and of great kindness, and repenteth him of the evil"* (Joel 2:12–13. Read also Isaiah 58:3; 2 Chronicles 20:15–37; 2 Chronicles 25:1–2; 2 Chronicles 32:24–31; 2 Chronicles 34:1–10, 19 and 27; Esther 4:1–4; Ezekiel 18:31–32 and Ephesians 4:22–23).

As we read these portions of Scripture, we see various examples of men and women of God who operated out of a perfect and an imperfect heart. Jesus wants repentance in this hour. As a Church, we need to repent from our sins. This is what is going to bring restoration and revival.

Is it possible to be renewed in our hearts and minds? This renewal is not just a "Sunday renewal"—what about persevering through affliction? What are we like? Do we say, like Job's wife, "Curse God and die"? Or do we say, "Though you slay me yet will I trust you"? God is calling the Church to search her heart in this hour. He wants to deal with every crevice. We have hidden enough; we have covered up enough. We have worn enough façades. We can fool some people, but God will have a people that we cannot fool and that will not be deceived. God is bringing us into a realm where we are going to know whether people are for or against us. We will have God's love to see right into people's lives.

That realm is coming; we are at its door. Are we prepared to give our hearts totally to God so that He can deal with us? Will He be able to use us for His honour and His glory in this hour? The only way God is going to be able to use His Church is if we repent. Peter repented because he saw where he failed the Lord. He wept bitterly for his sin. And so, God was able to use Peter mightily. Even the shadow of Peter healed people.

I believe that the realm we read about in Acts is coming back, but only as the Church seeks the Lord with a clean heart. This is going to draw the homosexuals, the lesbians, the drunkards and the backsliders back to church. Many churches are empty. Many Christians have nothing to offer.

Our lives are no different from the world. So we had better be real, because the world is seeking for reality. God wants reality from His people, from His Body. And, it is only the reality of God that is going to make the difference. We need the love of God in this hour, but it cannot be expressed through sin-laden lives. God is going to restore His Church. Are we willing to pay the price?

Repent ye therefore, and be converted, that your sins may be blotted out, when the times of refreshing shall come from the presence of the Lord (Acts 3:19. Read other references in Matthew 3:2,8; Luke 13:1–2 and Acts 8:18–22).

He is going to build His church and the gates of hell are not going to prevail against it. He is going to have a people that shall not bow to the beastly image of Baal. He is going to have a people called by His name. He is going to have a people that glorifies Him. David was a man who understood true repentance. This is why God called him a man after His own heart.

Create in me a clean heart, O God; and renew a right spirit within me (Psalm 51:10—read Psalm 51:9–17). If you have never been broken before the Lord, ask Him for that brokenness, so that you can repent before Him. Many times I cry before Him, because I recognize that I am in His presence. Who I am, and what is in my heart as I stand before Him, causes me to be broken. Isaiah saw the Lord—He was high and lifted up and His train filled the temple. Isaiah was broken because he saw the Lord; he said, "Woe is me, for I am a man of unclean lips and I dwell among a people of unclean lips." God is pleased when we are broken before Him.

Seek ye the Lord, all ye meek of the earth, which have wrought his judgment; seek righteousness, seek meekness: it may be ye shall be hid in the day of the Lord's anger (Zephaniah 2:3. Read also Matthew 22:37–39 and Zephaniah 2:1–2).

There are times when a message goes forth from the pulpit, or somebody ministers a word, and we become very stubborn. Or, we ask people to pray for surface needs, without getting to the real issues in our lives. We need to examine our hearts. Let us stop trying to impress one another. When we become truly honest with our hearts and learn to confess our problems openly, there is nothing more liberating. All of a sudden, the enemy can hold nothing over our heads. And it no longer matters what anybody says or thinks, because Jesus sees our hearts. He knows what's in there. He knows the little crevices and the skeletons in our closets.

What do you have in place of God? What high place do you have to tear down in your life? Don't feel bad—this is what it's all about. Tear down those high places, so that God can glorify Himself within our lives and say, "This is my beloved child in whom I am well pleased." Hear Him.

And rend your heart, and not your garments, and turn unto the Lord your God: for he is gracious and merciful, slow to anger, and of great kindness, and repenteth him of the evil (Joel 2:13—read Joel 2:11–17).

Do you see broken fellowship with Jesus? God's people are going through a lot of pressure in this hour. God is allowing the devil to bring us through the fire until we come forth like gold. He is going to burn the flesh off our bodies until only Jesus Christ is seen. Is it possible? Do you hunger for that? If so, then we can be His hands extended, reaching out to the oppressed. As we touch Jesus, we will touch those who are sick and afflicted.

Only then can we do it. Emotions are not going to do it. Excitement is not going to do it. Flesh is not going to do it. Only a broken heart, together with a surrendered life, will do it. Surrender all to Jesus. Let us not be afraid to let God set us free and to take out of our hearts whatever hinders us from moving forward. God wants to do it so He can glorify Himself within us.

Do you think that the Church has been a reproach? Yes, it has been: *"The heart is deceitful above all things, and desperately wicked: who can know it?"* (Jeremiah 17:9). But God tries the heart and wants us changed. He doesn't want us to come and go back the same way. If you think that you are spiritual, God wants to make you super-spiritual. Anything that you have today, there's more to strive for in God. None of us are walking in that realm. If we were, we would be doing the works of Jesus. So, there's room for work in all of us. There is a need for repentance in all of us. I hunger and thirst for Him. I want more of Him because I realize there is more. God is setting to do something supernatural. Let us not miss it. Let us not play Church. Let us not play Christianity. Let us be real.

This is an abridged version of this message.
Please contact us to order the tape of
this entire message.

Testimony: A Life Completely Healed from Mental Illness

This testimony is from a member of our church fellowship

The Lord Jesus Christ has been very gracious to me over the course of twenty-five years. He has brought me through many, many healings in my life—physical, emotional and mental healings.

I will be sharing mainly the effects of my mom's influence on my life. My mom, who has gone on to be with the Lord, must be very pleased to know that what the devil meant for evil, the Lord turned around for good.

My mom and dad had many problems in their marriage and personal lives. As a result, my mom became very frustrated and unwilling to be controlled by old-fashioned ideas, so she rebelled. When my oldest sister was born, my parents were separated; when I was born, my dad was in jail. They passed me between the bars of his cell so that he could see his new baby girl. My parents were both illiterate and only spoke Italian, which made things worse for them. My family came over to Canada from Italy in 1958. I was four years old, the youngest of three girls. As a young girl, I realized that my mom had mental problems.

Why do I say this?

- When she became angry with us, she would throw whatever was in her hands—even a knife. She pulled our hair, called us names, swore, talked about us while others were in our home and constantly cursed us, with curses like "As you give me trouble, so will you always have trouble."

- I remember once she had to change the sheets on our bed and it was really early, so she came and took them off the bed while we were still sleeping.

- She was very controlling, telling us to visit certain people, and used guilt to force us to go.

- When we wouldn't do what she wanted, she had fits and banged her head on the wall or fell on the floor and acted as though she was the victim.

I always felt sorry for my mom and wanted to be her protector. If anyone dared say anything about her in my presence, I defended her. I was obsessed with the fact that she did not know better and needed my help. I realized later on that my mom was suffering from multiple personality disorder. She was plagued with many physical and emotional problems. She was a very nervous person, had shock treatments, open heart surgery, a hysterectomy, suffered from depression and mood swings and constantly cried and felt sorry for herself.

Growing up, I was very quiet and melancholy, sickly and happy to stay in my room—a loner. I had no self-esteem, did not feel I was pretty and felt inferior to my friends and sisters. Rather than strengthen my weak points and work at who I really was, I created a false impression for the world around me. My negative turned into a false positive, my inferiority became a false security, my insecurity became pride and my fears became false strengths. I was really introverted—but extroverted for the world to see. I had fear of man, but showed no fear in public. To protect myself, I created a false character. My parents couldn't help us as we lived in two different worlds. They were always there to give us money if we needed anything, but rarely instructed us on how to cope in these situations.

I began to get terrible headaches from which sleep was the only escape—I slept excessively, so that time would pass by faster. I remember thinking of what I could join after school so that I wouldn't be the first one home, and while I was walking home from school, thinking what was going to face me tonight. These thoughts would come very often, therefore my childhood doesn't hold many good memories.

I hated myself so much. To get attention, I tried to excel in everything. I joined every sport and worked my hardest to be the best I could be. I was an excellent student, achieving honours throughout high school and never failing at anything. In turn, when I started working with people, they had to excel also or I would get very angry with them. I expected a lot from myself and from others.

As I began to go out with friends, I had a hard time fitting in. I felt that I had to constantly compete with them in order to feel accepted. This competitive spirit caused me to be aggressive, obnoxious and always looking to win at everything I did. This driven pursuit of perfection kept me from going insane in the environment that I lived in.

Years later, I found out through my psychologist that doing as I had done actually helped me to cope with who I really was. The Lord would divinely show me what I had done many years later, after I accepted Him into my heart. Not only did He show me—He completely delivered me from it all.

REPENTANCE BEFORE RESTORATION AND REVIVAL

My Pastor, Del Edwards, brought out an amazing study that the Lord had given her regarding the above subject (featured in this book). I realized, after hearing this study, that this was the process the Lord brought me through. First, there had to be recognition that I was not normal and that a lot of the things that I had done were sin. I had to recognize that I was not this "good little girl" I thought I was, but had suppressed a lot of emotion and hidden what I really wanted to say. Unlike my sisters, who were more vocal and honest about their anger, I hid it and made it seem like nothing bothered me. The Lord Jesus would show Pastor Del, in detail, how I had done this. When I realized what really happened to me and what I had done, repentance came.

This process took years; from 1980 until 1996, I was in shock and cried as I went through intense recognition and repentance. Pastor Del worked closely with me and one night even slept with me (as my husband did not know what to do with me and was so fearful). Her role was not easy, because she had to expose this false character by being hard on me. Then she would gently minister to me as I slipped into guilt, condemnation, self-hate, anger, hatred toward her for exposing my heart and self-sabotage. I wanted to stay in my house and do nothing.

So often, I felt that people did not understand. They

thought I was doing it for attention. I probably was, but I could not snap out of those moods until years later. Thank God that Pastor Del allowed the Holy Spirit to guide her and she had so much patience with me. She would have many, many dreams directing her to the next deliverance session. Many times she would have to wait for God to show her when to tell me, since the dreams were so horrible. Then, the Lord would give me a dream also, so that I would call her and tell her my dream and then she would tell me hers. It was so divine. She was dealing with many personalities in me (which I inherited from my mom), with the Holy Spirit as her only Guide.

RECOGNITION AND REPENTANCE—NATURAL

On my first date with the man who would eventually become my husband, I was so nervous when he kissed me that I vomited. We were married when I was twenty-two and my husband was twenty-four. At that time, we had a lot in common and we rarely fought. I had a great job as a buyer for a major supermarket chain. We had our own home, which we purchased and fully furnished before we were married.

On my wedding night, I began to feel mild symptoms of disorientation, depression and anxiety. Upon arriving in Acapulco on our honeymoon, I could no longer keep them to myself and had an all-out attack in one of the restaurants while we were eating. I began to have hot flashes, violent shaking in my body, dizziness, vomiting, diarrhea and pain in my left arm; being in dark places would bring on depression.

This continued after my return to Canada. We did not know what was happening to me. Sometimes I went to work feeling so sick that I would have to lay my head on my desk at times during the day in order to cope. When we would go out to eat, I would get these reactions. I then became very fearful of losing control of myself. I remember going to my husband's Christmas party; we were to have dinner at a hotel and then stay over for the evening. As soon as I picked up the spoon to eat my soup, I began to feel ill and we had to go to our room without finishing dinner. Things worsened as the evening went on; my husband sat up, watching me sleep, and finally had to call an ambulance since I was hyperventilating. Hospital visits began to be a common practice for us. I was thought to be pregnant or on drugs and was sent home because nothing showed up after medical testing. Finally, I went to Etobicoke General for a week of tests. They could only conclude that I had a nervous stomach.

One night, a very strange thing happened—this feeling of hopelessness and helplessness started to overcome me. I was cooking in the kitchen and felt like I had to run outside, but when I went outside, I felt like the air was engulfing me and I had to run inside. I felt trapped in this world, with no way out. I was so scared I rolled up in a fetal position on the floor and fell asleep.

The next day, I called my family doctor and was given a prescription for valium. Because I did not want to be medicated, my doctor referred me to a psychologist. This started a new journey. I had never told anyone about my home life. My two sisters talked to each other because they slept in the same room. I never joined in, although I remember my older sister constantly telling me that I needed to talk. I never would. It took me a few weeks to open up to the psychologist, a stranger, and even then I tried to protect my parents, telling him that they were illiterate and did the best they could. I remembered things I had thought were dreams, and as the doctor put them together for me, I began to understand why my body was reacting as it was. Talking to a psychologist began an incredible freedom for me. I saw him for two years and learned things about myself every time I went to see him, including:

- I had a false compassion for my parents.
- The claustrophobia from which I suffered was a result of feeling trapped in my home as a child.
- As a child, I had suffered shock and trauma. The human body has defense mechanisms to cope.
- I had to connect my feelings to my past experiences.
- Dreams could actually give clues to unlocking my past.

With every meeting I learned to cope with my body and emotions. I learned how to gain control over anxiety attacks and shield myself from depression and anything that I knew might be harmful to me.

I cried a lot driving home from the psychologist's office. I shared some things with my husband, but I knew he could not take too much, because he would worry. Then, after one and a half years of seeing this doctor, I came to know Jesus as my personal Saviour. I accepted Jesus into my heart and He began to take over my life.

I knew it was time to say goodbye to my natural doctor and give my spiritual doctor full control of my life. I did this with the encouragement of a prophet who visited our church. I had prayed a few times about when to leave therapy. That night, he came to me and said Jesus was going to take over and heal me now. I went home that night and said to my husband that I was going all the way with Jesus for my help. He was a little worried, but he had already seen a change in me, so he agreed. And so started the next phase of my life.

I dreamt that I was walking along a highway in the city where I now live; the wind was beating against me with such force that it took all the strength I had to push forward. I found my mother's house, where I saw her holding three bottles. Then she dropped one bottle on the floor. I knew that the Lord was showing me that I was free from my mother's control.

RECOGNITION AND REPENTANCE—SPIRITUAL

I thought the worst was over and that I was on my way to being healed. In a way it was true—I had begun the process, but the process became more painful and more intense. I now faced a supernatural enemy who did not want me to be healed. I learned that Jesus' process was not only to teach me to cope and learn how to control my anxiety attacks and depression, but He was going to remove them from me forever and ever! Can you hear me shouting? HALLELUJAH!

I attended a church that believed in the casting out of demons. These things that were in me—fear, abuse, anxiety, depression—were not from the Holy Spirit; therefore, they were from an evil spirit. The process of healing and deliverance is similar to childbirth—the woman is happy for the pains, for she knows that finally her baby is coming, but when the pain increases, the excitement goes away and all she feels is agony. For the next fifteen years, the Lord Jesus showed me one major deep secret in detail after another. He showed me a simple picture of what I had done, as a result of a study I was doing on pride for our prayer meeting:

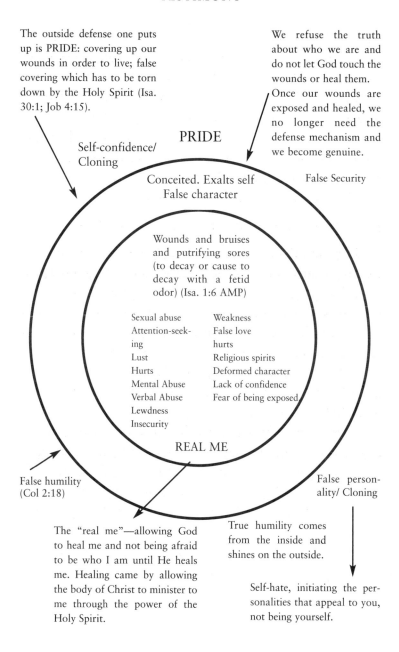

The outside defense one puts up is PRIDE: covering up our wounds in order to live; false covering which has to be torn down by the Holy Spirit (Isa. 30:1; Job 4:15).

We refuse the truth about who we are and do not let God touch the wounds or heal them. Once our wounds are exposed and healed, we no longer need the defense mechanism and we become genuine.

PRIDE

Self-confidence/ Cloning

Conceited. Exalts self
False character

False Security

Wounds and bruises and putrifying sores (to decay or cause to decay with a fetid odor) (Isa. 1:6 AMP)

Sexual abuse
Attention-seeking
Lust
Hurts
Mental Abuse
Verbal Abuse
Lewdness
Insecurity

Weakness
False love hurts
Religious spirits
Deformed character
Lack of confidence
Fear of being exposed

REAL ME

False humility (Col 2:18)

False personality/ Cloning

The "real me"—allowing God to heal me and not being afraid to be who I am until He heals me. Healing came by allowing the body of Christ to minister to me through the power of the Holy Spirit.

True humility comes from the inside and shines on the outside.

Self-hate, initiating the personalities that appeal to you, not being yourself.

As you can see, the outside circle is the false character and the inside circle represents the real me. It was this outside wall of pride that Jesus had to penetrate and break up and destroy. Then He had to take this inside circle, which was the real me, and strengthen it and make me to appreciate who I was.

The hard exterior wall I had allowed to form around my character caused me to become self-confident, conceited, and proud. I constantly wanted to be like others and actually cloned them. The first ones we recognized that I had cloned were my sisters. Later on, it was my sisters in Christ. Any character trait I liked, I "cloned." Pastor Del and I could actually hear the person speak out of me, or I would act like the person. I could not have seen any of this without the help of the Holy Spirit through Pastor Del.

This character I had built up to protect myself had to be destroyed. Every time it was touched, I would go into a "frozen state of stupor" for hours—sometimes days and months. With every exposure and deliverance, I was dying more and more to this outside shell and becoming more myself. At first, I did not believe Pastor Del as the Lord used her to expose who I really was, but I needed a divine intervention of His Spirit to deliver me. As a Christian, I prayed and fasted, trying to be as strict in the Word, baptized in water and Spirit-filled.

The Lord then started to deliver me from all of my inside shell of hurts, insanity, mental illness, schizophrenia, etc., and that's how I began to be restored to who I really was and begin to like myself. The Lord used His Word to strengthen my character and divinely linked me to His character.

How did God deliver me?

One of the first areas (nice word for "evil spirits") that the Lord showed me was jealousy. I had learned to write everything down so that I could remember to tell the psychologist, and as I was sitting in the service one night, the Lord told me to write down "jealousy, mother, sister." I began to get very angry. Many times in those early days, I would leave the church, burn rubber on the way out of the parking lot and go home. The church people got on my nerves and what they said made me sick.

I felt that my mother had favoured my middle sister. Then, I stopped the car and began to be sick to my stomach. I realized that the Lord was delivering me from this jealousy, and I allowed Him to do it. I felt so happy and excited and free after it was all over, and realized this was the Lord's deliverance.

Through deliverance you learn that spirits operate together. I found out that around the word "jealousy," other demons warped my mind. There was a competitive obsession, anger, fighting for position, and murder. It was very painful to deal with all of these areas, as the Lord used my sisters in Christ in certain situations to reveal my heart. Here are some examples:

- We would go out together for dinner; I would start off excited and happy to be with them, and end up feeling empty, rejected, frozen and in a stupor just because of what had been said.

- If I heard Pastor Del favouring other women, I withdrew from her and the women, wanting to be alone again, or I would get upset with them.

- Try as I might, I could not participate in their conversation, and if I had nothing to say and was getting no attention, it really bothered me.

One other example of the deliverance process can be seen from a time when we were in my kitchen praying for something, and my body was becoming limp and weak. Pastor Del asked me, "What is going on?" I told her that I felt weak and spaced out. She said, "You look like you're drugged—have you every taken any drugs?" Of course, I remembered the valium I had taken for many months, and we were shocked over what happened after that. The Lord began to deliver me from the valium still in my body, and after the deliverance I perked up and was fine. That's how real it is, and how personal the Holy Spirit can be.

One thing Pastor Del and I did was to talk, a lot. As we talked, the Lord would expose things to us. A major one was the fact that, like my mom, I also used a form of fit to get my way. When an area was exposed in my life, I would go into a "frozen state" where I wouldn't move or talk or lift up my head. This, we found out later, was for attention.

I repented, and I felt I had to make things right. When I met with Pastor Del and we prayed, the Lord delivered me from temper tantrums, curses, witchcraft, fits, attention-getting, etc. Then He spoke prophetically to me, through Pastor Del's life, to encourage me: "I will use you as an example. This is why I spent so much time with you, to use you in this hour. I will establish you and lead you into all righteousness. But, My Way is narrow. I have called you from your mother's womb and I love you with an everlasting love."

The dealings of the Lord became so painful that at times He had to use the supernatural realm to hang on to me. He showed me visions I could hang onto during the painful times. Here are some that I wrote in my journal:

Winter 1989 ...*The Lord was dealing with me regarding religious spirits and taking me apart inside. I was feeling guilty and condemned, and He was breaking away my old theology. As I was driving on my bus one day, I was so down about all these sins that the Lord was showing me. It was a very cloudy, windy day. The bus mirrors are very big and allowed me to see a lot of the sky above. As I glanced to the right I saw one little patch of the most beautiful blue just behind the black thick clouds and the Lord said to me this is who you really are. As you see all these black clouds you will see that underneath there is a pure blue you because of Jesus. As the winds would quickly blow the black clouds away He showed me that he would also take away my sins that I would be able to see more and more blue. When I went home I opened my Bible at this exact Scripture, Isaiah 44:22: "I have blotted out, as thick as a cloud, thy sins: return unto me; for I have redeemed thee."*

April 22, 1992 ...*I saw a vision while I was in prayer. I heard that He would give us the keys of the Kingdom. We then asked Him to open those doors. I saw a big castle with all this giant furniture. I saw a little girl trying to climb up a giant chair at a giant table and God was there and He was a giant too. I believe He showed me how great He is! I was there with Him as a little child and He would mature me.*

RESTORATION AND REVIVAL

I was raised up in my Christian walk through the Word of God. God used Pastor Del through dreams and He spoke to her through the Word of God concerning my heart. He gave her prophetic utterances about my life. The Lord used her to take me apart and to put me back together again. The Lord gave her much wisdom, and I learned to do good. He showed her how to be hard and how to be gentle and, after twenty-five years, we are still together.

God has been faithful to His Word and to me. Looking back over twenty-five years of ups and downs, ins and outs, we have gone through a lot together. The process at times almost separated us. I didn't think I could go on with it, and at times became hostile towards Pastor Del. She let me go once, and said if that's what I wanted, that was fine. Thank God, He never left us, and He kept us working together. He took a frail, weak, insignificant person and made a confident, strong, able person who can now help others, for no other reason than to work for Him and help His people. I now:

- have three children, a husband and a beautiful home;
- work as a head secretary at a school;
- sit on two different non-profit boards as a director;
- head fundraising for a missionary organization;
- teach children's church;
- sit on a fundraising committee;
- am in charge of outreach and evangelism for our church;

- pray with different people when asked;
- go on missionary trips.

I am able to do more today, at forty-nine, than I could do at age twenty-five, when I was loaded down with all those demons. I am very content and peaceful and am not overworked. When you work in the Holy Ghost, there is no striving, and if there is, we should back off, regroup, get prayer and go on.

I thank Jesus for dying for me and helping me every step of the way. I thank God for His Holy Spirit. I thank God for Pastor Del, who became a sister, brother, father and friend to me, so that I could be healed. I thank God for my husband and children for standing with me and loving me. I thank God for my blood sisters. I thank Pastor Neville, the congregation of Mount Zion and all of our sister churches for being there whenever I have needed them.

My prayer is that you will see how Jesus loves you and can take you and transform you; according to your faith, **He will do it.**

Chapter 5

Generational Curses

A t the end of 1997 and the beginning of 1998, the Lord spoke to me a tremendous revelation on generational curses. As He has often done, He spoke to me through a dream. In this dream, I saw engravings like gravestones, graves dating back to the 1700s. I saw a family name on my father's side, rooted in Scotland, and I realized that these represented generational curses that we have accumulated as a family. And I also realized that this was a timely message for the church.

Some may say that Jesus Christ died and we are saved and that we should be walking above disease and sickness. Well, obviously we are not there. There is something wrong and if there is something wrong, then we have to go back and find out what is wrong. Why are we sick as Christians? Why are we diseased? Why do we still have these problems if we are washed with the blood of Jesus and are now descendants of Christ, not Adam? It would seem that healing available in Jesus Christ escapes our grasp. So, I believe

God wants us to dig deep into our hearts, our lives, our families and cultural histories, so that we no longer walk around with sickness and disease, both spiritual and physical. The church often walks well below her privileges. God is trying to get to the foundation of what is causing us to move away from Him. I realized this as I studied the Word of God.

There are many areas in which we carry generational curses, sometimes unknowingly. It all began with Adam and Eve in the Garden of Eden.

> *And the LORD God called unto Adam, and said unto him, Where art thou? And he said, I heard thy voice in the garden, and I was afraid, because I was naked; and I hid myself. And he said, Who told thee that thou wast naked? Hast thou eaten of the tree, whereof I commanded thee that thou shouldest not eat? And the man said, The woman whom thou gavest to be with me, she gave me of the tree, and I did eat. And the LORD God said unto the woman, What is this that thou hast done? And the woman said, The serpent beguiled me, and I did eat. And the LORD God said unto the serpent, Because thou hast done this, thou art cursed above all cattle, and above every beast of the field; upon thy belly shalt thou go, and dust shalt thou eat all the days of thy life: And I will put enmity between thee and the woman, and between thy seed and her seed; it shall bruise thy head, and thou shalt bruise his heel. Unto the woman he said, I will greatly multiply thy sorrow and thy conception; in sorrow thou shalt bring forth children; and thy desire shall be to thy husband, and he shall rule over thee. And unto Adam he said, Because thou hast hearkened unto the voice of thy wife, and hast eaten of the tree, of which I commanded thee, saying, Thou shalt not eat of it: cursed is the ground for thy sake; in sorrow shalt thou eat*

of it all the days of thy life; Thorns also and thistles shall it bring forth to thee; and thou shalt eat the herb of the field; In the sweat of thy face shalt thou eat bread, till thou return unto the ground; for out of it wast thou taken: for dust thou art, and unto dust shalt thou return (Gen 3:9-19).

Because sin entered into man, he was cursed from the beginning.

Gen 5:3 says, *"And Adam lived an hundred and thirty years, and begat a son in his own likeness, after his image; and called his name Seth."*

Adam begat a son in his own likeness and after his own image. *"And, all have sinned and come short of the glory of God"* (Romans 3:23). Until Jesus Christ came, man lived under a continual curse. But Jesus Christ came to redeem us from the curse of the law—He paid the ultimate penalty. Jesus Christ became a curse for us in order to break our generational curses; that we might live truly free and victorious Christian lives. It states clearly in Deuteronomy 21:22-23 that everyone that is hanged on a tree is cursed. This is what Jesus suffered for us, taking on our curse that we might through His blood live free from our generational curses.

The problem with most of Christendom is that we do not fully appropriate the liberty afforded us at Calvary. It seems that we would rather walk with the curse of cancer, or heart disease, or witchcraft, or addictions and suffer the consequences of the sins of our forefathers, rather than search our family backgrounds, confess our faults and be completely delivered by the power of the blood of Jesus Christ. As I mentioned before, we live below our privileges because we do not fully understand the depths of Satan

(Revelation 2:24) or the power of the blood of Jesus Christ to truly liberate us from the shackles of our ancestral bloodline. When we are born again, we take on a new Father, a new bloodline—that of Jesus Christ. We must therefore renounce (2 Corinthians 4:2) all that preceded that new life and new ancestral heritage in order to walk in the complete healing afforded to every believer at the cross.

What are some of the key areas that Christians should examine when searching out their past? Well, everyone must go back to Adam (as we are all descendants of Adam) and renounce the Adamic curses pronounced in the Garden of Eden. And, we all have individual generational roots and curses because we were all born in different families, with different cultural backgrounds. For example, some of my roots dated back to Scotland through my father, and we must reach back to all of the generational and cultural roots and curses belonging specifically to the culture we were born in. We must renounce all negative aspects of our culture, our people, in order for the blood of Jesus Christ to set us completely free.

At a women's retreat, when we were ministering various messages on generational curses, one particular woman had a dynamic testimony. While at the retreat, she had testified how her mother had become pregnant out of wedlock at sixteen years of age and how she and all of her sisters had also become pregnant out of wedlock at sixteen years of age. She recognized that there had to be a generational root and curse that she had to renounce. While she was receiving deliverance for these generational curses, she could feel a cracking in her head, and she knew that God was breaking some things in her life. At the very same time, her children (grown son and daughter) who did not know what was happening to their mother at the retreat were experiencing the very same manifestations in their heads. This is the power of our God to deliver His people and their children!

Another critical area for Christians to receive deliverance is in the area of physical illnesses and diseases. When we go to the doctor, he/she will always ask us about our family history: "Did your mother have breast cancer? Did your father have heart disease?" etc. Why is that? It is because these curses are spiritually, and at times genetically, inherited through our natural bloodline. But Jesus Christ and His sacrifice on Calvary came to give us victory over all of our sicknesses and diseases. By His stripes we were healed.

> *Who his own self bare our sins in his own body on the tree, that we, being dead to sins, should live unto righteousness: by whose stripes ye were healed. For ye were as sheep going astray; but are now returned unto the Shepherd and Bishop of your souls* (1 Peter 2:24-25,24).

So, if we have a family history of arthritis, hypertension, heart attack, breast cancer, prostrate cancer, cancer, Alzheimer's disease etc., we must renounce all of these generational diseases inherited from our bloodline, so that the curse ends with us. We no longer have to die prematurely of all of these diseases and, more importantly, we no longer have to transfer these bloodline diseases to our children before birth. Jesus Christ has come to heal us!

There are also curses in the area of witchcraft. This is particularly true if our ancestry has been involved in witchcraft in any way. Even if we have never partaken in witchcraft activities or rituals, we can still be operating under an inherited area of witchcraft if there is any of that activity in our ancestry. Witchcraft comes in many forms: white/black magic, taro cards, psychic readings, tea leaf readings, idolatry (idolatrous religions and rituals), religious rituals, baths and salts, potions and spells etc. There are some false religions in many parts of the world that are also considered ritualistic witchcraft according to the Word of God. Also, going to a grave to ask the dead for ministry gifting is a form of witchcraft.

And, of course, the Lord tells us that rebellion is as the sin of witchcraft (1 Samuel 15:23), so any form of anti-submissiveness and rebellion to your parents, spouse, or to any established authority could be considered witchcraft. Again, I have to emphasize that partaking in actual rituals is not necessary to have an influence of witchcraft in our lives. If any member of our family's ancestral line has partaken in any form of witchcraft, we may well have inherited areas in this realm. No Christian easily admits that they are possibly operating in a familiar spirit or witchcraft, as opposed to the Holy Spirit, but it is important to ask the Lord for discernment and for Him to give us purity in all aspects of our ministry. He wants us to be completely free so that we can rest assured that we are operating in ministry through the fullness of the Holy Spirit and not motivated by impure familiar spirits. Even if we are unsure whether or not we have had witchcraft in our backgrounds, it is still important to renounce those areas and if there is any influence there, it must leave.

Another important realm for breaking generational curses is in the area of the mind. Many members of our congregation had inherited areas of depression, mental illness, schizophrenia, multiple personalities, dementia, absent-mindedness etc. Some areas of the mind not functioning properly may be related to several areas in our past. For example, sustained drug use, mental, verbal, physical and sexual abuse or a history of mental illness in our families could all be causes of mental problems that must be broken through the power of His blood. He has promised to give us the mind of Christ (1 Corinthians 2:16), but as far as the heaven is from the earth, so are His thoughts from our thoughts (Isaiah 55:7-9). The bridging of the gap between our human, sensual and devilish minds, to His Christ-mind is not complete just with reciting the sinner's prayer. It is a process through which God delivers us through the power of Jesus Christ, and changes our mindsets, our biases, our ways of thinking that are not aligned with His Word.

He promises us that all of those who love His appearing will see Him as He really is (1 John 3:1-3) and he who has this hope purifies himself, even as He is pure. It is only when God truly delivers our minds from all of its generational curses and inherited areas that we can truly begin to see God as He is (Matthew 5:8), not as we think He is, created out of our biases. When we relate God to what we deem Him to be based on our backgrounds and our upbringing, more often than not we turn the image of the Creator into the image of the creature (Romans 2:21-23). Let us seek to have the Lord cleanse our minds and set us free from our hang-ups and our mindsets, that we might truly know the Lord Jesus, just as He is. Sadly, many Christians serve "god," a "god" out of their own creation and mindset, who only exists in their own hearts, and they never fully come to the knowledge of who Jesus really is.

Other problems that can seriously afflict Christians are addictions. Addictions can take various forms, such as substance abuse (i.e. alcohol and drugs), addiction to food, television, gambling etc. These things can take control of our lives for many reasons. For example, if we have been raised in a dysfunctional family environment, we may be prone to addictions to fill unmet needs. We may suffer from self-rejection and, as a result, use food to fill the loneliness and rejection we feel. Or if a parent (or anyone in our ancestral lines) suffered from an addiction, then we too are prone to inheriting that proclivity and may become addicts ourselves.

When listening to testimonies on how God dealt with an addiction, we all too often hear that these individuals learned to "cope" with their addictions and continued to exercise discipline and self-control to overcome still present desires in that particular area. We listened to one testimony recently of a man who is a recovered alcoholic. He mentioned that there is not a day that passes that he does not desire a drink and that when the urge to drink overwhelms him, he screams out in anger. This is where the ministry of deliverance is very powerful. With deliverance, Christians do not simply "cope" or require continual counselling, but are truly set free from all desires and the battle against any addiction becomes a complete victory. No more mental gymnastics while we try to cope with every carnal, addictive desire, but through the power of the blood of Jesus Christ, every desire is removed, as though we had never suffered an addiction. This is true victory and true restoration. [See "Testimony: A Life Set Free from the Shackles of Alcohol]

The final example, (though there are many more) of a generational curse that must also be broken from our lives is a financial curse. Many of us live under of a curse of poverty and financial disparity. If we are doing what we must do as Christians (i.e. tithes and offerings), then the Lord Jesus Christ will bless us; this is His promise (Malachi 3:8-10). If we do not honour Him and His Word in our giving, then we are cursed with His curse. When God curses us, no man or prayer can break it. But when we are giving as we should according to the Word of God, and we are not prospering, we should dig deeper into our ancestral lines. Was there a thief, or someone who went bankrupt, or someone who gained money dishonestly in your bloodline? Did your family grow up in poverty? Did your father gamble? These curses can be broken by the power of Jesus Christ. The Lord does not consider gain as godliness, but He does promise to make adequate provision for His children. As David said, "I have been young, and now am old; yet have I not seen the righteous forsaken, nor His seed begging bread" (Psalm 37:25).

> For, behold, the day cometh, that shall burn as an oven; and all the proud, yea, and all that do wickedly, shall be stubble: and the day that cometh shall burn them up, saith the LORD of hosts, that it shall leave them neither root nor branch (Malachi 4:1. Read also Malachi 3:1-18; Malachi 4:2-6; Proverbs 30:8-14; Isaiah 58:6-14; Deuteronomy 7:21-26; Deuteronomy 29:1-21].

If we want to be blessed, then we have to do what the Word of God says. We close our eyes at important verses and hold on to those verses that look so beautiful and claim them. But unless we walk in all of the ordinances that God said we should walk in, then we are going to miss out. We can't expect to claim God's blessings when we have not done what He has asked us to do. He said, "I'm going to rebuke the devourer for your sakes." Then why aren't we healed? This is the Word of God and all of it is for us. It is for our benefit, but we must keep every part of it. We have to live according to that which He asks us to do.

When we have total deliverance, then we awaken in His likeness. As we walk in the valley, we learn to endure its quietness. Then we can walk on the mountaintop and have tremendous experiences. But we need to come back to the valley where we recognize Him in our valleys, where we walk with Him. It is in the valley of the depths of our own hearts where we really learn how to walk with Him.

God is a God of everlasting mercy. God does not destroy us; we destroy ourselves. We throw ourselves in Satan's hands and all Satan wants to do is steal, kill and destroy. God wants to protect us, but we take ourselves out of His protection and open up ourselves to the demonic realm. Jesus Christ comes to give us life. He cannot give us life if we do not abide in His Word (John 15:7). Jesus Christ has done everything He can possibly do for us at Calvary. Now, we need to appropriate it for our lives. He's a gentle Father and He has given us a new covenant to follow. We are not babes, we are no longer children, we are adults. He wants to treat us like mature children.

Then, as mature children, how do we remove these curses from our lives? In our ministry, we call it the "five Rs process." The first step is *recognition*—we must recognize that we have generational curses and research our family history and culture in order to know what we must renounce from our lives. Secondly, we must *repent*. We have to have a change in heart and attitude, and repent from the individual sins of our past and the sins of our forefathers in order for Jesus to bring everlasting change into our hearts. Then through the power of deliverance by the blood of Jesus Christ, we *remove* all of these generational roots and curses from our lives. Through the process of deliverance, Jesus Christ begins to *restore* each of us body, soul and spirit (1 Thessalonians 5:23), until we are made perfectly whole and are completely healed from our past. And the fifth and final "R" is *resurrection*, the place we come to when we begin to taste His resurrection power and come into the abundant living that He promises us in John 10:10. The truly victorious Christian life is not the covering of our sins, nor is it deliverance from difficult situations. But, it is the removal of our sins, so that we taste true freedom on the inside, in our hearts and deliverance in the situation. True victory is to have complete peace and rest in our problems, not after we have been delivered from them. Victory is on the inside, where no one sees and no one understands the peace we can enjoy, even through the most trying circumstances. This true victory can only be enjoyed when we have completely broken our generational roots and curses, by the power of His blood.

> *And make straight paths for your feet, lest that which is lame be turned out of the way; but let it rather be healed. Follow peace with all men, and holiness, without which no man shall see the Lord: Looking diligently lest any man fail of the grace of God; lest any root of bitterness springing up trouble you, and thereby many be defiled; Lest there be any fornicator, or profane person, as Esau, who for one morsel of meat sold his birthright. For ye know how that afterward, when he would have inherited the*

blessing, he was rejected: for he found no place of repentance, though he sought it carefully with tears. For ye are not come unto the mount that might be touched, and that burned with fire, nor unto blackness, and darkness, and tempest, And the sound of a trumpet, and the voice of words; which voice they that heard intreated that the word should not be spoken to them any more: (For they could not endure that which was commanded, And if so much as a beast touch the mountain, it shall be stoned, or thrust through with a dart: And so terrible was the sight, that Moses said, I exceedingly fear and quake:) But ye are come unto mount Sion, and unto the city of the living God, the heavenly Jerusalem, and to an innumerable company of angels, To the general assembly and church of the firstborn, which are written in heaven, and to God the Judge of all, and to the spirits of just men made perfect, And to Jesus the mediator of the new covenant, and to the blood of sprinkling, that speaketh better things than that of Abel. See that ye refuse not him that speaketh. For if they escaped not who refused him that spake on earth, much more shall not we escape, if we turn away from him that speaketh from heaven: Whose voice then shook the earth: but now he hath promised, saying, Yet once more I shake not the earth only, but also heaven. And this word, Yet once more, signifieth the removing of those things that are shaken, as of things that are made, that those things which cannot be shaken may remain. Wherefore we receiving a kingdom which cannot be moved, let us have grace, whereby we may serve God acceptably with reverence and godly fear: For our God is a consuming fire (Hebrews 12:13-29; 13. Read also 2 Chronicles 7:14-22; Isaiah 5:21-30; Zephania 2:1-7; Hosea 14:1-9; Matthew 15:10-13).

It is important that we not reject and misappropriate all that His blood has been shed to accomplish in our lives. He has given us His warning. He tells us who He is. He tells us that we are not going to be touched. We are not to be like Esau who sold out his birthright. He has given us opportunities, so that we can be healed. He has made provision. But He is warning us because He is a consuming fire. But the consuming fire that God wants to be for the church is to consume all of our generational roots. We miss out as a church and inherit things through sin, like sickness and disease. We walk around without joy. We walk around with condemnation and guilt and godless character. We move ourselves away from that which God has designed the church to walk in.

As we see the time approaching, we persuade men with the Word of God. This is a serious hour and we need to put on the whole armour of God. I believe it is later than we think. I want to take it seriously. Let's not just brush things off and say, "there is always tomorrow." Tomorrow may never come for you. It is time that we renounce our natural bloodline to Adam, with all of its curses. It is also time to appropriate our new bloodline, the royal heritage available through the blood of Jesus, with all of its blessings. There are generational blessings accessible to us through the provision of the bloodline of Jesus Christ, when we become His children.

And it shall come to pass, if thou shalt hearken diligently unto the voice of the LORD thy God, to observe and to do all his commandments which I command thee this day, that the LORD thy God will set thee on high above all nations of the earth: And all these blessings shall come on thee, and overtake thee, if thou shalt hearken unto the voice of the LORD thy God. Blessed shalt thou be in the city, and blessed shalt thou be in the field. Blessed shall be the fruit of thy body, and the fruit of thy ground, and the fruit of thy cattle, the increase of thy kine, and the flocks of thy sheep. Blessed shall be thy basket and thy store. Blessed shalt thou be when thou comest in, and blessed shalt thou be when thou goest out. The LORD shall cause thine enemies that rise up against thee to be smitten before thy face: they shall come out against thee one way, and flee before thee seven ways. The LORD shall command the blessing upon thee in thy storehouses, and in all that thou settest thine hand unto; and he shall bless thee in the land which the LORD thy God giveth thee. The LORD shall establish thee an holy people unto himself, as he hath sworn unto thee, if thou shalt keep the commandments of the LORD thy God, and walk in his ways. And all people of the earth shall see that thou art called by the name of the LORD; and they shall be afraid of thee. And the LORD shall make thee plenteous in goods, in the fruit of thy body, and in the fruit of thy cattle, and in the fruit of thy ground, in the land which the LORD sware unto thy fathers to give thee. The LORD shall open unto thee his good treasure, the heaven to give the rain unto thy land in his season, and to bless all the work of thine hand: and thou shalt lend unto many nations, and thou shalt not borrow. And the LORD shall make thee the head, and not the tail; and thou shalt be above only, and thou shalt not be beneath; if that thou hearken unto the commandments of the LORD thy God, which I command thee this day, to observe and to do them: And thou shalt not go aside from any of the words which I command thee this day, to the right hand, or to the left, to go after other gods to serve them (Deuteronomy 28:1-14).

When we serve and obey Him, and allow Him to have access to the recesses of our hearts, there are many blessings afforded us. And He wants us to let go of our generational curses and enjoy His generational blessings. Once we surrender to Jesus Christ, the Lord is quick to reward us with His joy and peace (Revelation 22:12-17). And it is a peace that the world cannot understand.

This is an abridged version of this message. Please contact us to order the tape of this entire message.

Testimony: Deliverance from a Dysfunctional Upbringing

This is another testimony from a member of our church fellowship

The focus of this testimony is to talk about the process of God in making me truly Christian. The process of becoming truly honest with the heart is a journey. It is a journey I walked with Jesus and I thank God, with a trusted pastor who refused to speak anything but the truth into my heart. I was born in a large family and I was not a wanted pregnancy. I was born with a lot of rejection and that root of rejection has hindered me a lot through my walk and dealings with this heart. Every time the Lord corrected me, I felt rejected and it has taken many years to come into a clear understanding.

This journey began in 1990, I was saved for three years at that point. We went away to ladies' retreat, and at that retreat, I had a divine encounter with the Lord. I remember the Lord's presence so thick in my room, as He was flooding scriptures into my spirit that I literally felt as though my flesh would explode. I knew that in this flesh, I could not stand such an outpouring of His presence and His glory.

Years later, in the thick of my trials and my process, I cried out to the Lord and repented over and over again because of the agony I was in. He spoke to me at that time, "Daughter, I want to talk to you, I want to commune with you and how can I when you have so much sin? I cannot fellowship sin and I want to fellowship you, so allow me to cleanse you from that which keeps us apart." This is why He has chosen to work with my sinful heart and to change it, so that we could enjoy unbroken communion one with another, as Adam had in the garden.

In 1990, I also began to travel on the mission field during my vacation time and this is where I received most of my correction and training. I joined a youth ministry as Youth Director, because I liked how the title sounded when I was on the mission field and Pastor Del would introduce me... I thought it gave me credibility. I thought I was so holy and righteous and that I was God's chosen messenger and that His work could never advance without me. My thoughts were evil continually, against my pastors, against my brethren, but I never spoke them. I just kept up "appearances." I remember receiving prophecies that I loved God's people, and I knew that deep in my heart, I had not come into that reality, I only loved myself.

The process of coming into this kind of honesty took a long time with me. Imagine that you are going to the nations to preach the gospel, twice, sometimes three times a year and you operate out of jealousy, envy, strife and contention, all in the heart and thought life. People, your brethren, can't stand to be around you because you behave in such ungodly ways. So, how did God work with me? Well, He raised up Pastor Del. We were taught about deliverance, that we were all born in sin and shapen in iniquity and that Jesus Christ could set us free from our sins. I had addictions to cigarettes, I swore, I lied, I had a spirit of alcoholism, inherited from my father. And I understood that Jesus Christ died for those sins and that He could set me free. So, deliverance at first, the process of laying on of hands and the manifestation of Satan as he leaves your body (coughing up in my case, though there are many manifestations) was great at first. I felt light and free, because I no longer wanted these hang-ups in my life. Then, the Lord touched on sexual areas, thoughts/fantasies, dreams, perversions and that became a little more difficult. That was so embarrassing and how could I share these dark things openly with anyone? But God gave me the grace and Pastor Del was never condemning, in fact, it was so matter of fact with her that it was a great relief to speak it openly to someone I could trust. The Lord also dealt with hurts from my past, as my father was an alcoholic and I never knew or understood the love of an openly affectionate father. In all these things, I was the victim and it was relatively "easy" to get deliverance and to feel free.

But then the real process of honesty began, where it was no longer what others had done to me, but what I had freely chosen and what I had done to others. I had to deal with those actions that I was completely accountable for in His sight. This kind of honesty hit who I was as a person, the very core of my being. That process began as Pastor Del would have dreams about me, about my character. She would see my heart completely naked in a dream. At first, I would resist, I could not understand why God would show her my heart and not me. But now I understand that we vitally need the body of Christ, especially the fivefold ministry to perfect the saints for the work of the ministry. I realize even more that we cannot be objective about our own selves. We need others to see for us and that takes a tremendous amount of trust.

To enlarge on that, I remember that she had a dream that we were travelling together on the mission field and that we were sharing a room. We were supposed to share a bed, but when she came to sleep in the bed, I had soiled the bed with runny diarrhea. When I heard that dream at first, I was completely devastated. There was no way I could be that bad, that dirty. She patiently shared and prayed that God would open my eyes to the truth. But, during that counselling session (which can take hours), she said one thing that really impacted me. She simply said that I needed to be healed. I thought I was okay. What did I need healing from? When I went home after that counselling session, I was crying in my bed and I said, "Lord, what do they see? How do they see me?" And then I finally heard what Pastor Del was trying to say to me about my own heart. At that time, I saw myself the way I wanted to be, not the way I actually was. The world saw me the way I actually was, which is why I always felt that no one really understood me. But the reason why I felt that no one understood me is that the world saw what I really was, so in fact, it was I who did not understand myself. But, the Lord was in the process of changing all of that. I began to see that I was really hurting, that I had a lot of mental problems that I had to work through. I was mentally unstable even though I had gone to graduate school and accomplished a lot and had a good, solid job and some assets and lived a responsible "Christian" life.

In order to be free from something, it was important for me to get to the root cause and to understand what motivated my behaviour. Sometimes I would be ministering on the mission field. I remember Pastor Del having a dream that I had false hair or by interpretation, a false anointing. The devil knows how to flow in false gifts and if we are not honest with our hearts, we can flow out of a sensual and familiar spirit and not the Holy Spirit at all. So, I had to get deliverance from cloning other ministries and false anointing. How? Pastor Del exposed my false works, and she sat in a counselling session and shared what God showed her. I had to take in the correction and receive it and believe it. That was the most difficult part, especially when you think you love the Lord and when you think that you are being effective for Him. Then I had to renounce those works of darkness by verbal confession "I renounce a false anointing" and so on. Then my sisters laid hands on me and took authority over the specific sin I was struggling with by the blood of Jesus. Christians can't have spirits? That has not been my experience and I know no other way that really worked for me to be truly healed. I tried to fake healing and it never worked. I tried to work up faith and it never came. I was crying out for reality on the inside, to be impressive to God not to man, because He sees everything. So, when you pray those kinds of prayers, please expect that He will reveal all that is false and fake and a facade and a show. Please expect that the process will be painful at times.

In 1998, I came back from a mission trip to England where I had a lot of struggles with my thought life, particularly against Pastor Del. The enemy would always attack my thought life with respect to Pastor Del, because God was using her the most to help set me free from all my problems. And I hated when the thoughts would come, and I would rebuke and rebuke Satan, with little power, little victory. The reason? Because I was not honest. Finally, Pastor Del confronted me and said "Why don't you just admit that you hate me? Just say it, Del I hate you!" That was very shocking to me, because I thought that I loved her. So I drove home that night and I prayed "Lord, what evil is in me, what terribly wicked thing is in me that I cannot respond to such love as has been poured into my life over the years from such selfless people, who only want my good? How is it that I can be so hateful, when others have sacrificed so much to see me healed?" That evening, I was lying in my bed and a memory came back to me that I had completely forgotten. When we were children, we had several cats and our cats would sometimes have kittens. One summer, I remember that we were playing with this kitten and we were doing very mean things to this sweet little animal. In the end we killed it.

Then, an avalanche broke in me. What kind of person was I really? The capacity to kill a sweet innocent animal! That's when my eyes started to open that something was seriously wrong with my way of thinking, with my upbringing.

I renounced all of those past sins that tormented me and influenced my behaviour. If there is one thing about this ministry, there is absolutely no point trying to pretend to be someone you are not. We may as well be honest with what is happening inside and expose it. The Lord sees everything and He wants us to be real inside and out, more than we do!

I went away that weekend and did not realize that God had only begun to deal with this area of truth and how I made choices despite the somewhat neglected upbringing I had come under. At the beginning of the year (1998), Pastor Del had a word for the church that we needed to break our generational curses (featured in this book). I had a dream not long after that, and I was rebuking some young people about how they were treating a classmate and I said, "you have the wrong foundations." So, as I was away, I happened to be reading a book that weekend and that opened my eyes to the lack of correction that I had received in my home. My parents rarely corrected me. I was not really taught love or trained how to give or how to behave with grace. I made the choice to be rude and aggressive and belligerent, like a dog.

When I came to that reality, I realized that I had been raised with the wrong foundation and that, through my choices, I had become completely dysfunctional. I had to completely renounce the negative aspects of my culture and any mean-spiritedness that exists within that culture. One morning, we were praying for another sister and I made a "joke" about some of the sensitivities of her heart. Well, it wasn't funny and it served to open my eyes that much more. I realized that it was the only way I knew how to interact with people because of the choices that I had made and I realized how warped my behaviour was. I had to repent to my sisters and brothers in Christ for having to put up with me all of these years, my belligerence and my complete lack of love, my cruel jokes intended to be funny, but which only brought pain. I had to look back on times when I would minister from the pulpit on the mission field and a spirit of anger would rise up in me to rebuke God's people. What I thought was the anointing was a spirit of condemnation and meanness, wanting to slam God's people down. I wept many bitter tears.

I was not kind, giving and charitable with my thoughts and deeds. On the surface, I was able to fool most. But I could not fool God or the Holy Spirit in His true servant. I had to deal with the anger I had against my parents. I understand now that they did the best they could, but as a young person, I made a lot of angry choices that brought consequences. It was not until I began to understand His love through observing a truly loving family, where I could never fit in, that my eyes were opened to the truth about myself, and the choices that I willingly made. And did that truth ever go a long way to setting me free! From that point, I was able to completely turn my character around, with God's people praying for me, and His Word. I would observe every comment, the ways in which I interacted with people to tease or put down. And, I worked diligently to change those habit patterns in my life. Deliverance is only the first step. Then, we have to walk it out, through prayer, fasting and the Word of God to keep our deliverance.

Afterward, Jesus findeth him in the temple, and said unto him, Behold, thou art made whole: go and sin no more, lest a worse thing come unto thee (John 5:14).

It has been sixteen years and I know that I continue to endeavour to walk whole in all of the things that I have mentioned above. Also, God dealt with something that has completely changed my life. I was listening to a message ministered by Pastor Del on the wilderness and I thought that I had some divine inspiration during the message. I mentioned to her that she sometimes preached the message with such simplicity that people might possibly misunderstand the depth of what she was saying. And she told me the next morning and explained that the message of the gospel is simple, a simple Word, a simple message just to be believed. All I was doing was complicating it in my mind and it was losing its effectiveness to heal me. That was a divine encounter. I then sat through a counselling session to deal with problems I had around the mind and intellect. Motives in my heart that I wanted to be seen and heard with such divine revelations—whether they were false or not. I had to renounce intellectualism, being overly analytical, relating to God's Word through intellect and not by the Holy Spirit. All of a sudden, I realized that His Word is so simple and simply to be believed. It lifted many things from my life, such as condemnation.

To this day, whenever the enemy wants to bob me up and down like a yo-yo, I recognize that the Word of Jesus Christ is real to uplift, to support and to heal. It is there as a plumb line, a lifeline, a sword to see us through each moment of the day. I no longer go to the Word thinking that I have a divine ministry calling, looking for the word for the hour. Now, when I read the Word, it is in a simple relationship, relying on its truths to bring me higher into Him. What a wonderful place to trust Him and prove Him at His Word.

I have heard it preached by some that it cannot take a long time to heal, and if it does, something is wrong. But I can only speak from my own experience. When we began this adventure we were charting new territory. I did not realize how many layers the Lord would have to unravel. At first, it was very difficult for me to accept that someone else could be raised up to so plainly see my heart. It was difficult for me not to resist this person speaking to me, because I did not immediately recognize that it was Jesus using His body to speak to me. Then, as the process went along and the Lord was digging deeper into my character, its flaws and its motives, I had no sense of who I was, only an endless sense of sadness and pain. And I wore it on my countenance; I could not lift up my weak hands and feeble knees. But Pastor Del was there, trying to encourage me, trying to convince me that all of this correction was the love of God and His great favour. There were times during the process that I had nothing in my prayer, so I would just sit and scream and cry and scream some more. It was as though the Lord had turned His back on me, and I did not feel His love.

This brought about a feeling of bitterness and hatred toward the Lord, of which I am ashamed. All of the things which I thought He had promised me were dung and all that was left was me and having to come to the realization that my heart was evil and that I needed to change my heart, my mind and my entire life. These were not lifestyle changes, like not drinking or smoking, these were changes that were required in the very recesses of the heart. Many times, I would cry myself to sleep or walk around like a zombie because I did not know who I was or who I would become. But, our light afflictions are not worthy to be compared with the glory that shall be revealed in us.

He was there all the time, lovingly changing me to know Him. Today, I feel whole and complete in many areas, and I am striving as Paul did, for the prize of the high calling of God in Christ Jesus. When I say "I love you" to someone, it is no longer mere "Christian words." When I say "I forgive you", it is no longer because I know 'it's the right thing to do', but rather these words flow from a sincere heart of love,

His true love on the inside. As Christians, as I have learned, we can all talk the talk and to some extent, walk the walk. But in the deep recesses of my heart, I knew I was a fraud. I could speak such eloquent words, was faithful in attending meetings/services, travelled the nations to share the gospel, and worked in fundraising and other activities. I thought I was giving my all to the Lord. But when He started requesting that I really give my all, that's when the real test of love and faithfulness to Him began. I have failed Him in more ways than I can adequately express on these few pages, but He has replaced my failures with His great loving kindness. His blood was shed not just for me to pray a sinner's prayer and seal my trip to heaven. His blood was shed to take someone like me, someone who made choices and acted without graciousness, only rudeness, bitterness and hatred. His blood transcends time and reaches into the deepest part of this heart to change me.

Many have said, "you weren't that bad"... but I know the pit He dug me from. That's what was difficult for me through this process. There were many around me saying "you're so sweet, you really love the Lord, you are an example etc." And, then I had my counselor, Pastor Del, saying, "you need to be honest, you need to come clean, you need to admit you have problems, you need to change!" If for one moment I was tempted to listen to all of the other voices, I would have missed where God has brought me today. That stern voice of correction was His voice, and above all, deep inside, He put the desire for total truth inside, even though it hurt every time it came to confront me. Truth offends, but if we can receive it, it also sets free and we are then free indeed!

I believe that part of the reason why most of the church resists this kind of testimony is fear of exposure. If someone who appears to have it all together and who appears to really love the Lord can make these kinds of confessions, I am sure some think "what about me? What will I have to confess?" And, that very thought is enough to frighten most away from the process. That's why the Lord excludes the fearful from the kingdom (in Revelation). And this is why many, maybe even you, say that this can't be God. Dismiss it, don't deal with it and dance around under the "anointing", only to realize when you come face to face with a Holy God that you fall far short of your calling. I don't want to know the truth about His assessment of my works on that day; I want to know now. If I am lightly esteemed in His sight, I want to know and to make it right.

What have I learned in all this? That His Word is true when He says that He has raised up the fivefold ministry to perfect the saints for the work of the ministry. Pastor Del's life is a testament to that scripture. That His Word is true when He says whom He loves He chastens and that it does yield the peaceable fruit of righteousness if you are exercised by that chastening. That His Word is true when He says that He will forget our iniquities and remember our sins no more. He died to remove our sins and iniquities and to give us the power to walk as He walked, above sin. I have learned to love Him and trust Him in a realm that I never thought possible. I realize that what I thought was a deep and abiding love before this process began was only puppy love. Now, when I say yes to Him, I understand what it means. I have learned that His Word is true when he says that weeping may endure for a night, but joy comes in the morning. But the most important thing I have learned is that all things do work together for good to those who are the called according to His purpose. I have lost many things, but what I have gained in return is more powerful and priceless than anything He has asked me to lay down. He is true to His Word and He uses His body to transform lives. If we can abase ourselves to receive and understand that, He will one day exalt us.

This year for me has been the loosing of my captivity from my many prisons. Walking in truth, body, soul and spirit. To know that you are free on the inside and that your mind is no longer tormented... Who can put a price tag on that? I am sure Pastor Del joins me when I say that I have many miles yet to travel, but everything that we have endured together on this journey so far has been worth it all. May I learn to love Him more and to continue to serve Him with an increasingly purer heart. Amen.

Our soul escaped as a bird out of the snare of the fowlers: the snare is broken, and we are escaped. Our help is in the name of the Lord, who made heaven and earth (Psalm 124:7-8).

Chapter 6

Now Is the Time to Take the Kingdom

This is an abridged version of this message. Please contact us to order the tape of this entire message.

A the end of 1998, I had three dreams. In the first dream, the Church was lame and diseased in the feet. I was prophesying that it was a heart condition—not a natural sickness in the feet, but a heart condition. When our hearts are not functioning the way they should before the Lord, our walk becomes a problem.

In another dream, I set up an appointment with the President of the United States and he was ready to be cleansed in his heart. He mentioned having a generational curse, but was ready to be set free.

On Christmas morning in 1998, I had a third dream, that we were in England and there was a choir singing at a church that I recognized as one that we had visited on a missionary trip. I did not, however, recognize anyone in the choir. They were singing,

"Now is the time to take the kingdom; rise up, be strong, possess the land, For every power and dominion is given now into your hand, ye that have ears to hear the trumpet, ye that have eyes to understand. Now is the time to take the kingdom; rise up,

91

be strong, possess the land."

As they sang, I was supposed to stand up next to speak. The thought came to my heart that the choir did not understand what they were singing. Then I realized that we speak and sing these great, swelling words, and really don't even know what we are talking about or singing. Then came a profound message for the Church, that now is the time to take the Kingdom.

I realized, as I studied Scriptures on this topic, that the Old Testament prophesied about Jesus' coming. John reflected on the Kingdom; Jesus Himself preached that the Kingdom is at hand. We know that before John, Jeremiah and Isaiah and all of the great prophets foretold the Kingdom. We know that John and all the prophets ministered and foretold of God's Kingdom. And Jesus, when He came, preached the same message: the Kingdom of God is at hand. For 1999 I heard all that was happening, with the introduction of microchip technology input in human beings and a lot about the year 2000 and many things that are now happening. Let me tell you, however—just as the enemy is doing his thing, God is doing greater things in the Church. I am truly excited, because it is time for the Church to stand up. He has come and it is not a weak Kingdom.

Many of us know the Scriptures, but are they real in our lives? It is time that we appropriated what God has intended to do. I am truly excited. It is time that the Scriptures stop being quoted and become reality in each of our lives.

"The time is fulfilled, and the kingdom of God is at hand: repent ye, and believe the gospel" (Mark 1:15). This was Jesus speaking. He came to demonstrate the power of God. We are not talking about an external kingdom that will set up a prime minister. I believe my dreams showed that the Church is lame

and that God must set us free. There is a kingdom of darkness in our hearts; Jesus has come to set us free from that kingdom of darkness and establish His Kingdom in His Church. Before He sets up His Kingdom here on earth—and He will do this—He must establish His Kingdom in our hearts.

When Jesus came the first time, it was the fulfillment of all that had been prophesied before. We have preached the gospel of the Kingdom, but we have preached it with weakness and have not seen the demonstration of the power of His Kingdom as Jesus Christ taught it. But it is God's time, and rather than frustrate ourselves, we need to understand His time clock and prepare for what God is doing now in the earth. Jesus wants us to prepare our hearts so that the Kingdom of God can be enlarged in us.

"For the kingdom of God is not in word, but in power" (1 Corinthians 4:20). The Kingdom came with demonstration of power. Have we seen power in the Church? I believe that we are moving towards it. God has moved slightly; we have had little waves of revival here and there. But I know the Church is not going out weak. I know that, with what is happening in the system and Satan's kingdom, we need more than we have today, and I know that this is preparation time. God is going to restore the Church to her fullest. His Kingdom is coming forth. Now is the time to take the Kingdom. When God speaks to me through dreams, I go with brute force. I know that God has spoken, that now is the time to take the Kingdom. Why? Because the kingdom of darkness is establishing itself—how much more the Kingdom of God? The Church must come into her full maturity, the fullness of all that God has prepared for her.

Which is a manifest token of the righteous judgment of God, that ye may be counted worthy of the kingdom of God, for which ye also suffer (2 Thessalonians 1:5).

Looking at the Church for a quick moment, I know that there is a deposit in us. I know that the Holy Ghost is that deposit in us. Now, Jesus Christ has left to go to the Father, and He has sent the Holy Ghost, which is that Kingdom. I tell you that the Lord spoke to me some time ago that the Church would be likened unto Job. This hour, the Church is going to go through physical ailments. When everything is going right, we can all praise the Lord. When things unravel around us, are we going to praise the Lord?

He showed me that Satan will touch our physical man. He spoke to me, sometime ago, to fear no evil. And if He says not to fear evil, this means that evil is coming, evil is here. The one thing that will defeat the Church in this hour is fear. So, we need to get rid of fear, because when we have fear, faith cannot operate. We need to band together as the Body of Christ and fight for one another. We have to determine, when Satan attacks our bodies and our families and our finances, we have to realize that God permitted all of this. How are we going to function when all of these things happen? I am speaking out of experience; Satan has attacked my family and my finances and my body. God was testing my reaction in the trials. God trusted Job that he was going to stand through the trials. *"Though he slay me, yet will I trust him…"* (Job 13:15a).

To whom also he shewed himself alive after his passion by many infallible proofs, being seen of them forty days, and speaking of the things pertaining to the kingdom of God (Acts 1:3—read Acts 1:1–8).

The Church has been talking about the Kingdom of God being at hand for over 2,000 years. And we know that the

Kingdom of God is within us, which is the Holy Ghost in us. The Lord showed me that there are two kingdoms, the kingdom of darkness and the Kingdom of Light, and we are in the process of dispossessing the kingdom of darkness and possessing the Kingdom of Light. This is Christ coming forth in our lives, bringing us into maturity, making us sons in His image. Let us not fool ourselves—either we take the kingdom of darkness or the Kingdom of Light—there is no in-between. This Holy Ghost, this Kingdom, is power within you. This is what God has called the Church to be: a witness in our homes, in our jobs and in our neighbourhoods and to the uttermost part of the world, that Jesus Christ will be seen in our lives.

"But if I with the finger of God cast out devils, no doubt the kingdom of God is come upon you" (Luke 11:20—read Luke 11:17–20). Do you want to know what the Kingdom is all about? Read the life of Jesus Christ and the lives of the disciples. You see, Satan has established his kingdom in our hearts, but he cannot stay if we have determined in our hearts to cast him out. Authority, rule, reign and domain—this is what Kingdom means! Are we ruling? I believe it is coming. This is why, I believe, I had the dream about the President of the United States. That will not necessarily happen in the natural, but the Church is going to reclaim her rightful place. I am telling you, Church, let us get rid of all of the kingdoms of the enemy and let the Kingdom of God possess our being!

The Lord showed me that the restoration He has for His Church is a process, just like deliverance is a process. This is all part of the process of God that He has been taking us through. So, finally, after 2,000 years, God is saying, "It's time to take the Kingdom," and it's time to stand up and be counted for God. It is an exciting hour.

Chapter 7

War a Good Warfare

This is an abridged version of this message. Please contact us to order the tape of this entire message.

While travelling in England in November 1999, I had a dream that a man was trying to kill me. I knew that I had to kill him first. Remember, the Word of God says the enemy has come to steal, kill and destroy. He says, "I have come to give you life, abundant life" (John 10:10b). I knew in my dream that the enemy wanted to destroy me, but I knew that I had to destroy him. Finally, when he saw that he was losing the battle, he killed himself.

From that dream, I realized that the Church is going to have to fight more than we have ever fought before. I am talking about spiritual warfare. I think the Church is going to get blamed for many things, and certain communities will put pressure on the Church for certain rights; it doesn't matter, because His Word is going to come to pass. We have to teach our children how to fight as well. The enemy will use their friends to pull them away from that which we have invested in them.

This charge I commit unto thee, son Timothy, according to the prophecies which went before on thee, that thou by them mightest war a good warfare" (1 Timothy 1:18. Read also 1 Timothy 1:19; 1 Timothy 2:1–3 and Romans 7:23).

The title of this message is "War a good warfare." The first thing we need to deal with is spiritual conflict; we need to deal with our own inward battles. Once we have conquered them, it is going to be easy to fight. This is one reason why we struggle. This is why our youth struggle, because there is a lot of warring inside. Jesus Christ has come to set us free, so that we can walk free. For us to fight a good warfare, we must first deal with the inward self, and we can only fight spiritual warfare in the Spirit.

For though we walk in the flesh, we do not war after the flesh: (For the weapons of our warfare are not carnal, but mighty through God to the pulling down of strong holds;) (2 Corinthians 10:3–4; read 2 Corinthians 10:3–7).

When disobedience comes, when the devil wants us to go the other way, we must be ready to recognize it and to make war. He is trying to move us away from the obedience of the Word of God, from doing what is right. He is an invisible foe, but we see his effects in the world. Our God, however, is greater than him. It is only going to get more difficult as we see the day approaching, but God is going to equip His Church to fight. This battle was won at Calvary, but we have to appropriate that victory to our lives.

For we wrestle not against flesh and blood, but against principalities, against powers, against the rulers of the darkness of this world, against spiritual wickedness in high places (Ephesians 6:12. Read also 1 Timothy 6:11; Hebrews 10:32–35; Revelation 1:1–3 and 12:17).

This warfare demands complete devotion. It demands complete consecration, not a wishy-washy commitment. We can only be perfected through Him. We need to start fighting for this body. We need to start redeeming this body that God has given us. It is important to know we have the power within us, because Jesus Christ is there. Our confidence is not in ourselves; it is not in the physician, it is not in the hospital—it is in Jesus.

As a Church, we often talk about hearing the Word, but very little about keeping the Word in our hearts. There is a Church that is preparing to meet Him, and there is a Church that is sitting back and waiting for something to happen. There is a remnant seed that keeps the commandments of God and the testimony of Jesus. In order to have this testimony, His Word has to be kept in our hearts. *"Thy word have I hid in mine heart, that I might not sin against thee"* (Psalm 119:11. Read also Romans 10:8 and Colossians 3:16).

That Word has to be kept by faith in our hearts. It is time that we stop speaking our own words. It is time that His Word be in our hearts as a priceless treasure and that out of that treasure, life would flow from our hearts to help others.

We must learn to pray this Word into our lives. So often, we have fancy words and can pray the roof off of a church. Unless we pray the Word of faith, however, we have not prayed at all. The Word of faith is Jesus Christ through His Word. We have to eat this Word, fully digest it and use it to fight the Enemy. When Jesus fought the devil, He said, "It is written." We have taken this Word too lightly. God is going to have a remnant that will go out with His Word, that two-edged sword which destroys the works of darkness. The devil knows this, and he is going to make war with that remnant. So, as Paul admonished Timothy, war a good warfare and enjoy complete victory in Jesus Christ.

Chapter 8

Now, Give Me This Mountain

I woke up one Saturday morning while I was away in England to Joshua 14. When I returned from England, a sister called me. She was not well. As I prayed for her, I was praying this message that God gave me. When God gives you a message, it's fresh in your soul and you are excited about it.

> Now therefore give me this mountain, whereof the Lord spake in that day; for thou heardest in that day how the Anakims were there, and that the cities were great and fenced: if so be the Lord will be with me, then I shall be able to drive them out, as the Lord said. And Joshua blessed him, and gave unto Caleb the son of Jephunneh Hebron for an inheritance. Hebron therefore became the inheritance of Caleb the son of Jephunneh the Kenezite unto this day, because that he wholly followed the Lord God of Israel (Joshua 14:12–14).

In every congregation, in every place, I believe there is a Caleb, and we need to cry out for this Caleb spirit. It does not matter how powerful the mountains may be—if Caleb can take it, so can you. When the Lord drops a message in my heart, I'm excited. I am excited because God speaks. What is important to me is that I am delivering that which God has given me for the hour in a fresh and living way.

> *And they told him, and said, We came unto the land whither thou sentest us, and surely it floweth with milk and honey; and this is the fruit of it* (Numbers 13:27—read Numbers 13:17–27).

I believe God wants to break strongholds. Whatever your problems are, whatever your sickness may be, whatever the doctors have said, we must stand on His Word. This Word is the Truth; this is reality, not the doctors, not what you read in the newspaper. This is Truth, the Word of God. The devil is setting up his messengers to bring fear. One of the things that harnesses God's people is fear, because Satan paints a big picture and he makes himself look more powerful than God. This is what he does in our minds. We forget that God delivered us out of Egypt. Satan is a liar and a deceiver and he will try to do everything he can to move you away from the hope of the gospel. He did it with the children of Israel, and he will try to do it with us.

We have too long felt sorry for ourselves, when we serve a great big God. We have a Mighty God, who created this universe, who dwells within us, and yet, we are afraid of the devil. Let's stand on our feet and fight him. Let's take out our weapons and destroy him. We can do it, Church, because Jesus Christ makes the difference in our lives. There is no reason why we should walk a defeated life. If you are walking a defeated life, it is because Satan has taken advantage of you. Jesus Christ has destroyed him, yet he is going around as a roaring lion seeking whom he may devour. He is *only* a roaring lion.

Whatever our mountains are, we have to possess them! The Word of God says, "You can speak to the mountain." He has given us the power to do it. One of the problems with the Church is that we do not believe we have power. We are still running around looking for faith. Where is faith? We have faith because we have Jesus in our hearts. How many times has God fought our battles and we have won? Why is it that when we are going through the trials and struggles, we cannot rejoice? We need to stand when we are going through the trials.

Show me your Christianity when you are going through the trials. Can we say, like Job, "Though He slay me, yet will I trust in him"? Church, we need to wake up in this hour! This is the time the Church needs to rise and claim her inheritance. Jesus Christ died and shed His Blood on Calvary. What more can He do? He has given us His life—what more can He do for us? May the Lord forgive us for not recognizing all that God has done for us. What glorifies the Lord is when we stand in the trials and say, "Lord I'm going to praise You."

Where are the Calebs in this hour? Let's have them, Church. Let us get rid of all that clutters our hearts, so that the Lord can use us for His glory. Sometimes we want the evangelist to do it for us; we want the prophet to do it for us. We want the pastors to do it for us. But we need to rise up, Church.

Pardon, I beseech thee, the iniquity of this people according unto the greatness of thy mercy, and as thou hast forgiven this people, from Egypt even until now. And the Lord said, I have pardoned according to thy word: But as truly as I live, all the earth shall be filled with the glory of the Lord (Numbers 14:19–21—read Numbers 14:1–21).

Sometimes we would rather die than fight, but God has provided a Body to minister to you. If you are in a church and that Body cannot minister to you, then find another church. We spend hours with our people, those whom God has given us, to pray for them. This is the responsibility God has laid on our shoulders. It is going to take a church; it is going to take a people.

It's not easy to work with people. You have to have the grace of God, and if you are willing, God will give you the grace. He loves His people. He rebuked Moses when Moses did not obey His commandments. Moses did not make it into the Promised Land, but Joshua and Caleb did. We need to pray for our leaders, because we do not want them to preach to others while they become castaways—and that includes me. We need the grace and the love of God.

Please understand the point that I am trying to make: God is here, not in person, but in His servants. He was with Moses and Caleb, and it was through them that He was speaking. And when the Israelites murmured against God's servants, it was God they were touching, because He heard them. Sometimes we think we are irreplaceable. If we do not obey Him and His servants, however, God knows how to replace us. He said He would raise up the stones to praise Him. He does not want to replace us and cause us to miss out, because He created us in His image for His glory and for His praise. He loves His Body, but He does not love rebellion. And when we rebel against Him and His Word, when we rebel against one another, we rebel against God.

When God raises up His Body, He expects us to listen. God is speaking His Word through His servants, and we need to hear. So often we run away from what God is speaking, run somewhere else to hear something else. We do not really want to deal with our hearts, because circumcision is painful. God is going to do a circumcision of the heart. He is purging our hearts, cutting away the foreskins of our hearts. When you go through the process of deliverance, God circumcises your heart. So whatever you have in your heart, just allow the Lord to circumcise it. I am not talking about the heart that pumps your blood—I am talking about the part of your heart where the soul is. He wants to take the evil out of our soulish nature, to make us whole and make us like Him.

> *The Emims dwelt therein in times past, a people great, and many, and tall, as the Anakims... (That also was accounted a land of giants: giants dwelt therein in old time; and the Ammonites call them Zamzummims; (Deuteronomy 2:10 and 20—read also Deuteronomy 1:25–30).*

It does not matter how great the giants are in the world, God will deliver us from them. Is there anything too hard for God? What giant can stand in our way when we are children of the King? We must conquer the giant of unbelief. There are a lot of giants in the Church. Fear, unbelief and doubt are warring and rampaging in the Church. This is why we are not moving on.

> *Hear, O Israel: Thou art to pass over Jordan this day, to go in to possess nations greater and mightier than thyself, cities great and fenced up to heaven, A people great and tall, the children of the Anakims (Deuteronomy 9:1–2).*

The Lord had given them the land, and they were going to possess it. But they forgot so quickly. So quickly we forget the work God has done, that God has delivered us and done a mighty work within our hearts. That He has saved us from an accident or saved us from destruction or saved our children. Tomorrow we are faced with another challenge and we quickly forget.

> *And now, behold, the Lord hath kept me alive, as he said, these forty and five years, even since the Lord spake this word unto Moses, while the children of Israel wandered in the wilderness: and now, lo, I am this day fourscore and five years old. As yet I am as strong this day as I was in the day that Moses sent me: as my strength was then, even so is my strength now, for war, both to go out, and to come in. Now therefore give me this mountain, whereof the Lord spake in that day; for thou heardest in that day how the Anakims were there, and that the cities were great and fenced: if so be the LORD will be with me, then I shall be able to drive them out, as the LORD said* (Joshua 14:10–12; read also Joshua 11:16–23; Joshua 14:6–9 and 13–16).

We can destroy a life with a bad report. We can destroy a church with a bad report. It is so important that we have a good report, and it is important that we keep the good report—because the report we have is the Word of God. The Lord also has our inheritance. It is not just a natural inheritance, but a spiritual inheritance to possess the Christ. As David said, "I will not be satisfied until I wake in his likeness."

> *Till we all come in the unity of the faith, and of the knowledge of the Son of God, unto a perfect man, unto the measure of the stature of the fulness of Christ* (Ephesians 4:13).

If you are imperfect, God can make you perfect. I am not talking about impediments—I am talking about spiritual perfection. I am talking about being like Jesus. Putting on His Nature, His Character, His Life, and putting off everything that is of the flesh. Putting on the Lord Jesus Christ and having no confidence in the flesh, that's what I'm talking about. We have that to possess. Unless we can walk above sin, walk possessing the Christ, then what good are we to the Lord? What glory are we to Jesus?

Come on, Church—we need to put on Jesus. Everything about Jesus is lovely. Everything that is good, everything that is of a good report, He says, think on these things. The fruit of the Spirit is everything that is love, joy, peace, longsuffering, gentleness. So, where is the Christ? Where is the fruit of the Spirit? We need to be delivered, Church. We need to be delivered until we walk like Jesus, until we purpose in our hearts that we want to be like Him. That is our goal. I don't know about you, but that is my goal. I want to do everything that pleases Him. I am not there, but I'm pressing forward. I purpose in my heart that today, if I make a mistake, I will not make it again tomorrow. We have to start preaching to ourselves. Put on Jesus.

Caleb was a man with a good report. Church, a good report gives health, gives life, gives vigor and excitement. Be excited… Christians live longer! People who go to church live longer. Why? Because we have the joy of the Lord. Glory to Jesus. Caleb says, "Now therefore give me this mountain." He was ready to take the mountain at eighty-five years old. Glory to Jesus. There are other examples of victorious faith. I want to show you some people of God. The first one is Abraham.

And he said, Lay not thine hand upon the lad, neither do thou any thing unto him: for now I know that thou fearest God, seeing thou hast not withheld thy son, thine only son from me" (Genesis 22:12—Read Genesis 22:8–18).

You might say that Abraham was just faking it, but God knew Abraham's heart. He was a man willing to give up his son. Father God has done that for us through Jesus; He has given up His only Son for us.

He gave His only begotten Son so that we might have life today, yet we still walk defeated lives. We need to change, Church. We need to change, and one person can make the difference. God sometimes puts us through the test. God allows the devil to put us through the mill, to see what is in our hearts, to show us if we are going to allow Him to cleanse our hearts. This is the Old Testament, and Abraham was a man of faith. This is God's voice to the Church right now. Many times we run to get a word. But I say, let me get a word from the Word of God. It is powerful.

> *And Jonathan said to the young man that bare his armour, Come, and let us go over unto the garrison of these uncircumcised: it may be that the Lord will work for us: for there is no restraint to the Lord to save by many or by few* (1 Samuel 14:6).

God is not concerned with the majority or the crowd. He says, "One can chase a thousand, two can put ten thousand to flight." He does not care about numbers.

Let's look at David, 1 Samuel 17. I am just showing you some men of faith in the Bible.

> *Thy servant slew both the lion and the bear: and this uncircumcised Philistine shall be as one of them, seeing he hath defied the armies of the living God"* (1 Samuel 17:36—Read 1 Samuel 17:32–50).

We need to know God for ourselves. David knew his

God, and was not going to depend on Saul's armour; he was going to depend on God.

We need to know God and trust Him. Sometimes we trust man more than we look to God. There are times when you will be on your own. One of the hardest times for a person who is sick is at night, because the devil will fill your mind with everything under the sun. Every disease is yours! This is how the devil will plague you. But those times that we are alone, we need to fight. The Bible says to resist the devil and he will flee. We need to resist the devil because Satan wants to destroy our lives. It does not matter what the storms are— God is going to come forth.

We serve the same God who delivered David. That same God will fight our battles. I am not saying it is easy. It is never easy. We have to draw from our Source, which is Jesus and His Word. It is not easy when our children go astray. It is not easy when our husbands or wives are not saved. But God is greater than our needs. Whatever they are, He will encourage us. He will be there for us. He said He will never leave us or forsake us. He will fight our battles. He wins all battles in which He fights. The Lord will build a hedge around us when He sees that we are weak. He will allow the hedge to come down, however, when He wants to show us something in our hearts. Do not be afraid of the trial, because it comes to make you strong, to glorify the Lord. So, whatever you might be going through, say like Caleb, "Give me this mountain," because it is God who is going to fight the battle for you.

Let us look at Jehoshaphat, 2 Chronicles 20. Our Bible is full of great messages.

O our God, wilt thou not judge them? for we have no might against this great company that cometh against us; neither know we what to do: but our eyes are upon thee (2 Chronicles 20:12).

We need to fix our eyes on Jesus. Whatever the problem is, let us not fix our eyes on the problem, but fix our eyes on Jesus. David did not see the giant, he saw God. He knew God and that was enough for him. He knew that God would fight his battles. Jehoshaphat was the same. Let us look at Job 19:25—*"For I know that my redeemer liveth, and that he shall stand at the latter day upon the earth."* Job did not know anything except that he had lost everything, and yet he said, "I know that my redeemer liveth." Job should be our example. When Job went through all that he did, he said, "Naked I came into the earth, naked I will go back." He did not hold back and there was no fear. He gave himself to God wholly. He knew that somehow God was going to see him through.

Let us look at the three Hebrew boys in Daniel 3.

If it be so, our God whom we serve is able to deliver us from the burning fiery furnace, and he will deliver us out of thine hand, O king (Daniel 3:17).

Here are men that had no fear. We have to prove God. God wants to do something supernatural. Come on, draw from Him!

Let us turn to a New Testament Scripture about the life of Paul:

On the morrow, because he would have known the certainty wherefore he was accused of the Jews, he loosed him from his bands, and commanded the chief priests and all their council to appear, and brought Paul down, and set him before them (Acts 22:30—read Acts 22:24–30).

Paul was not afraid. He wasn't afraid. So often we walk around with fear of man, fear that they are going to kill us or excommunicate us. We should not be afraid—it is the world or the devil that should be afraid of you. They were afraid of Paul.

> *And Paul, earnestly beholding the council, said, Men and brethren, I have lived in all good conscience before God until this day. And the high priest Ananias commanded them that stood by him to smite him on the mouth. Then said Paul unto him, God shall smite thee, thou whited wall: for sittest thou to judge me after the law, and commandest me to be smitten contrary to the law?* (Acts 23:1–3.)

Paul knew the law. We need to know this law. We can only fight the enemy with the law, with the Word of God. And many do not know the Word. Many wait for Sunday mornings; our Bibles collect dust and become part of the furniture. We need to know the Word to fight the devil in this hour. If Jesus, the Son of God, used the Word to defeat the devil, what do you think we should be using? But how can we use the Word if we do not know it? We need to write this Word in our hearts. We must hold it in our hearts and use it against the enemy. If we fight with our own words, we will be defeated. But use the Name of Jesus, His Blood and the Word, and we will destroy the enemy. All we need to do is draw from His Kingdom. The Lord has already fought for us at Calvary. The battle is already won. We only need to rise up and take our place in Him.

We are going to talk just a moment about health promised to the obedient believers. If your mountain is a mountain of sickness, health is promised to you:

And there shall be a great cry throughout all the land of Egypt, such as there was none like it, nor shall be like it any more. But against any of the children of Israel shall not a dog move his tongue, against man or beast: that ye may know how that the Lord doth put a difference between the Egyptians and Israel (Exodus 11:6–7. Read also Exodus 8:22–23; Exodus 9:6 and 26).

God protects His people. Are we His people? I believe this realm is coming. I believe we have moved away from the Word of God. I believe we are not seeing that which God has promised us because we are not walking as He tells us to walk. He is committed to His Word only as we obey it.

"And the blood shall be to you for a token upon the houses where ye are: and when I see the blood, I will pass over you, and the plague shall not be upon you to destroy you, when I smite the land of Egypt (Exodus 12:13).

Now, Jesus Christ has given us His Blood. There is a spiritual application of the blood today. In the Spirit, we sprinkle the Blood of Jesus over our lives by faith. We need to ask the Lord, constantly using His Blood.

Who is like unto thee, O Lord, among the gods? who is like thee, glorious in holiness, fearful in praises, doing wonders? (Exodus 15:11—read Exodus 15:11–25).

Only Jesus can take bitter things out of our hearts. Many of us have bitterness and we need to release it. The bitterness in our hearts will bring us further down and throw us further into Satan's territory to destroy us. Many times we hold on to our anger and malice and only hurt ourselves. The quicker we get rid of those things, the better off it is for us. Many times God wants to prove us, but we fail. He is a merciful God—why do we want to fail Him all the time? Why are we not willing to change, so that we can help someone else? Be a Caleb—take the mountain! We need to encourage one another in the Word of God.

> *And the Lord will take away from thee all sickness, and will put none of the evil diseases of Egypt, which thou knowest, upon thee; but will lay them upon all them that hate thee* (Deuteronomy 7:15).

Wow, are we excited? We do not have to fight our own battles. When I was growing up, people used to say that my father was in witchcraft. They could not believe that God was so real and could do mighty works that He used my father to do. Many times, people tried to do witchcraft on my father and the same curses they would send would come back on them. People used to say that my father was doing witchcraft. God's power is greater than the devil and no man can curse you. If God is for you, who can be against you?

> *A thousand shall fall at thy side, and ten thousand at thy right hand; but it shall not come nigh thee* (Psalm 91:7. Read also Proverbs 4:20–27; Proverbs 3:13–26).

Today every earthly soul, Christian or non-Christian, wants to be a millionaire. There is a treasure greater than finances, which is Jesus. *"The love of money is the root of all evil"* (1 Timothy 6:10), and it will kill us. Nothing can replace Jesus. *"It is easier for a camel to go through the eye of a needle, than for a rich man to enter into the kingdom of God"* (Matthew 19:24).

If riches increase, set not your heart on them. It is what we do to get money that is often wrong. Our confidence must be found in Jesus. I am confident because of Jesus. I was once afraid of man; I was a very shy and fearful person and had no confidence. Thank God for Jesus who has changed me.

> *And he answering said, Thou shalt love the Lord thy God with all thy heart, and with all thy soul, and with all thy strength, and with all thy mind; and thy neighbour as thyself. And he said unto him, Thou hast answered right: this do, and thou shalt live* (Luke 10:27–28. Read also Psalm 3:3–8).

We can boast in the Lord. Recently I dreamt the enemy was chasing me. There was a cleft in the rock, carved out especially for my body. I was in the cleft of the rock, and in the dream, I was certain the enemy would see me. But they passed by and did not see me. I woke up and I was so excited. Jesus is a personal God. He is tailor-made for you to fit your body into Him.

> *Although the fig tree shall not blossom, neither shall fruit be in the vines; the labour of the olive shall fail, and the fields shall yield no meat; the flock shall be cut off from the fold, and there shall be no herd in the stalls: Yet I will rejoice in the Lord, I will joy in the God of my salvation. The Lord God is my strength, and he will make my feet like hinds' feet, and he will make me to walk upon mine high places. To the chief singer on my stringed instruments* (Habakkuk 3:17–19. Read also Psalm 18:1–3; Psalm 20:7; Psalm 23:4; Psalm 27:3–4; Psalm 46:2; Isaiah 12:2–3 and Hebrews 3:11–19).

The Word of God does not guarantee eternal security if we do not obey and hold fast our confidence. This is the

New Testament, not the Old Testament. Stand on the Word of God, stand firm on His Word. God does not want us to cast away our confidence.

> *Let us therefore fear, lest, a promise being left us of entering into his rest, any of you should seem to come short of it. For unto us was the gospel preached, as well as unto them: but the word preached did not profit them, not being mixed with faith in them that heard it* (Hebrews 4:1–2).

The opposite of confidence is a lack of faith.

> *Then Jesus answered and said, O faithless and perverse generation, how long shall I be with you? how long shall I suffer you? bring him hither to me* (Matthew 17:17—read Matthew 17:17–21).

So, whatever your mountain is, I know that the Lord has given us this Word. I know some are going through situations that seem insurmountable. If some are facing some difficult challenges, like Caleb, you can take that mountain. If Caleb can take it at eighty-five years old, *we* can take it. God is not like man; whatever our mountains are, the Lord intends us to conquer them. It does not matter what the details are—God is able to deliver. The Blood of Jesus goes deeper than anything. Just trust Him to give you the victory!

This is an abridged version of this message. Please contact us to order the tape of this entire message.

Testimony: A Life Set Free from the Shackles of Alcohol

This is a final testimony from another member of our church fellowship

I was an alcoholic and a drug user. I drank a lot; I could not begin to tell you how I managed and how I functioned. My two children were two and four years old at the time. I had an identity crisis, and became very frustrated with my marriage and all that went with it. I got up in the morning and all I could think of was when I could take my first drink, to find my escape and make the pain go away. Drinking every day and night did not satisfy my need or make my problems go away, so I started to escape in drugs. It started with smoking marijuana and hashish; then I tried a chemical called acid, and after that, cocaine. My marriage was not working and I didn't want to try anymore, so I asked my husband to leave.

We have a government support system that will assist single parents with children. I lived and survived in this welfare system for several years. I was in bondage to the devil. My life was cursed; I was in bondage to welfare, and could not get out of the rut I was in. I was in bondage to alcohol and drugs, and I lived each moment of my life in fear of the devil. I had made the devil my companion. I saw him in every shadow, every dark moment in my life. He fed my loneliness, rage, anger towards my husband. I had thoughts of murder, wanting to pay my husband back for all that he had done to me, leaving me alone to raise two young children, abandoning me, although I did ask him to leave. My heart was full of wickedness and I just wanted to hurt someone.

I studied many different religions, reading many books, opening up myself to theories and theologies. I studied witchcraft, learning not only the history of witchcraft, but the 'how to.' In addition, I read every fiction and nonfiction book on the occult that I could get my hands on. I would feel every word that had been written in them begin to grow in me. I was addicted to it. I felt stimulated by what I read and felt the need to fill my life with more. I hungered to be fed with more books, movies and anything else I could get my hands on. This led me back into the drugs of my youth. The devil had a hold upon my life. I see now that I had opened my life up to the devil's devices—he now had a stronghold and kept me in the bondage of fear.

While under the influence of drugs and alcohol, I watched television. It became a vehicle the devil used to feed my needs. The drugs enhanced my awareness and brought me closer to the demonic realm. I could see images in the shadows. I remember when, under the influence of drugs and alcohol on one occasion, a friend and I heard a noise in the basement and proceeded down the stairs to investigate. We saw a movement in the shadows—the black silhouette of a man running down the stairs. This was real; not only was I possessed, but my home was a haven for the devil and his demons. Several years later, a visitor in my home came up from the basement with fear on her face and reported she had seen the figure of a man in black. I tell you this not to frighten you, but to make you aware of the devil and his devices.

It's not surprising that I had so many hang-ups in my life. I was looking in all the wrong places for a solution for my pain and I took refuge with the devil—not only hurting myself, but my children and those around me as well. At the time, I knew I was only surviving and thought what I was doing was normal. I conformed to the way of media influence and what was acceptable to the ways of the world, not to God.

I had so much anger and violence in my life. I entered into another medium of the devil's influence, the martial arts. I became very determined and driven; I had found a means to release my hostility on others. I practiced punching and kicking not only at the gym or dojo, but on my family at home. On one occasion, I was so frustrated with my marriage and so angry at my then-husband that I picked up an armchair and tossed it at him. The violence and aggression was increasing in my life; practising martial arts compounded an already bad situation. I was at the club every day and some nights. I couldn't wait to spend more time in meditation, the search for an inner peace, the place of rest and strength. I searched and searched, and was only led into a world not of our Lord Jesus Christ. The devil had control over my life and I let him have it.

I met a lady who became my friend. She radiated something I had never seen before. When I met her, I thought she had something I wanted. I had studied different world reli-

gions all through my life—Islam, Hinduism, Zoroastrian-
ism, all the '-isms' you could think of. I was raised a
Catholic, but I knew that I didn't have all that I needed. I
was lost and just looking for something that was missing in
my life. I developed my own theory of one God, one religion. That God came in different forms for different cul-
tures, with different names. I thought I had religion nailed
down pretty well.

But this friend was too good to be true; I was challenged to read the Word of God, not to see what she had,
but to prove that Jesus Christ could not be the Son of
God. I thought I had a handle on religion and understood
the whole theory of creation. So now I was all studied up
and had read the Word of God, and felt I was equipped
to challenge her and her God. I began to prepare my
debate with her, and to my dismay, discovered that Jesus
Christ was in fact the Son of God. *"And they shall call his
name Emmanuel, which being interpreted is, God with
us"* (Matthew 1:23). There was no contradiction—the
Word was truth. I was fully persuaded. I had no battle—
it was over.

For the first time in my life, I truly felt alive. I knew I
had to go to church and be with fellow believers, and that's
when God began to change my life. By the grace of our Lord
Jesus Christ, He pulled me out of bondage and started to
clean my life and set me free.

Through this process I found that the Lord had divinely set me free from the desire and want of drugs, but I still
struggled as a Christian with my addiction to alcohol. I
could not shake the desire, the want and need of a drink of
alcohol, beer or wine. The devil did not want to let me go.

I did not want to let it go. The Lord started to reveal, through the life of Pastor Del Edwards from whom I received counsel, the areas in my heart and life that kept me in bondage to alcohol. We began a process together, with assistance from other members in the Body of Christ, to pray for the delivering power of Jesus Christ to set me free from the things in my heart and life that kept me in bondage to alcohol. We prayed for the removal of the spirit of loneliness that was lingering in my daily life. I was brought into an understanding that the drugs and alcohol were a dependency and were feeding my loneliness. The Lord touched my life and delivered me as He released, one by one, the spirits of loneliness, rage, anger and hatred. This process was not a quick fix, but took place over a period of time, teaching and bringing me into an understanding of the Word of God.

I resisted on many occasions and tried to run away from what God was doing. The pain was too great and I did not want to deal with it or even look at my wicked heart. The Lord was patient and kind; Pastor Del never gave up, in spite of my resistance and my rebellious nature. The Lord prevailed. He delivered me and set me free. On many occasions I actually felt the releasing of the evil spirit (demon) through my hands. My hands would tingle and I would continue to shake them until I felt it leaving my hands. The power of prayer to cast out these demons was the beginning of a new, purified walk. It was possible to be free and not bound.

Now that I was free from the spirits of loneliness, hatred, anger and murder, I wanted the alcohol to be gone from my life. I despised it and what it had done to me. One evening I came into the church service and I could smell alcohol all around me. Everywhere I went, I could smell it, even in the seat I was sitting in. I could not shake it; the temptation was all around me. My insides were turning and my mouth began to water with anticipation of a drink. I began to feel really sick, like I wanted to throw up. I was very restless and anxious and I wanted to be set free. I did not want this demon tormenting me anymore. I did not want it in my life. I wanted to be free.

At the end of the service, I spoke to Pastor Del and she called on another sister in the Lord so that, together, they could agree in prayer that the Lord would deliver me from this tormenting demon. Immediately, they took authority in the name of Jesus Christ and I began to cough. The ladies stayed and prayed with me until I felt totally free.

This took place approximately eleven years ago. **I am not a recovering alcoholic—I am completely free.** I do not desire a drink. I no longer need a drink; the spirit of alcohol has completely left my life. I have been restored, delivered and set free by the Blood of the Lamb.

Now that the Lord had opened my eyes, I could see why I was such a mess. He was preparing to clean my life to make me whole, removing every spot and wrinkle of sin from my heart, such as witchcraft, the occult and fear. This portion of my testimony is a reflection of my life before my deliverance. Yet, I must explain, this is a process of working out my salvation with fear and trembling before the Lord. I strive to have everything out of my life that is not of God. As each wicked layer of my life was being peeled away by the Lord, the Lord began to reveal other things I had touched.

There is so much more I could share. The Lord's delivering power has set me free. I have much to be thankful for. I am a miracle—a living testimony of what Jesus Christ has done. He has set me free from, alcohol, drugs, hatred, anger, murder, fear, witchcraft and much more. I am a single parent with two children. At the time of writing, I was employed with an internationally known company in the food industry, and the Lord has blessed me tremendously, giving the increase in my life. He is my peace; He has broken down every wall. I owe everything to Him. This is why I have dedicated my life to serve the King of kings, Lord of lords.

Chapter 9

Maintaining Your Deliverance

I love the Word. One of the things that will deliver us in this hour is His Word. And this Word that will deliver us is the same Word that will sustain us.

> *When the unclean spirit is gone out of a man, he walketh through dry places, seeking rest; and finding none, he saith, I will return unto my house whence I came out. And when he cometh, he findeth it swept and garnished. Then goeth he, and taketh to him seven other spirits more wicked than himself; and they enter in, and dwell there: and the last state of that man is worse than the first. And it came to pass, as he spake these things, a certain woman of the company lifted up her voice, and said unto him, Blessed is the womb that bare thee, and the paps which thou hast sucked. But he said, Yea rather, blessed are they that hear the word of God, and keep it* (Luke 11:24–28. Read also Luke 10:18–19).

Jesus beheld Satan and He knows that he is a defeated foe. But Christians can have unclean spirits within and these demons must be cast out of our lives. Then, when the enemy is gone, the Kingdom of Light has come. But Satan does not give up territory easily, and he will always roam around us to cause us to slip into our old ways again and again. And he comes back with seven worse than the first.

How do we avoid him finding us empty? We must be filled with the Holy Ghost. And, we need to pray, fast, read the Word and be nurtured by the Body of Christ.

Put on the whole armour of God, that ye may be able to stand against the wiles of the devil (Ephesians 6:11; read also Philippians 4:13; 1 Peter 5:6–10; Romans 13:12–14; 2 Corinthians 6:3–10; 1 Corinthians 10:12–14 and Hebrews 2:18).

One thing I must establish is that temptation is not sin. But when we yield to temptation, sin comes in. If the enemy tempts us, we know he is trying to gain entrance back into our lives. The Word of God warns us and prepares us so that we can recognize our adversary, the devil. So, we maintain our deliverance through the Word. We must not allow anything to replace the Word of God. We have to go into our closets and search the Word for ourselves.

Because thou hast kept the word of my patience, I also will keep thee from the hour of temptation, which shall come upon all the world, to try them that dwell upon the earth (Revelation 3:10. Read also 1 Peter 2:1–5 and 1 Thessalonians 5:17).

Pray without ceasing. At one time, my husband lost his job in a company where he had worked for years. He called me to let me know, and I would not allow the enemy to bring fear. I was driving along the road and I just said in my heart, "Lord in the name of Jesus, You can reverse this situation." When I got back home, the phone rang and my husband said, "They have reversed the situation."

Sometimes we get so traditional and ritualistic about prayer, but prayer is communion with God. Does God know your heart? Praying is not only necessarily praying words—sometimes praying is just singing a song. Many revelations I have had were through prayer. Prayer is the key that unlocks many doors.

> *Confess your faults one to another, and pray one for another, that ye may be healed. The effectual fervent prayer of a righteous man availeth much* (James 5:16; read also Isaiah 58; Ephesians 6:16–18; Acts 2:42; James 4:7; 1 John 4:4).

There is a victory found in submitting. It's not always easy to submit, because we want to have our own way. But we cannot resist the devil until we submit to God. Greater is He that is in us. *Who* is in us? JESUS!

Remember, maintaining our deliverance is the least that we must do. There is more beyond mere maintenance. There is a realm of walking above sin.

I am talking about perfection, holiness, righteousness, and becoming mature sons of God. Many churches preach to just accept Jesus and enjoy our salvation. But there is more.

> *But if ye be without chastisement, whereof all are partakers, then are ye bastards, and not sons* (Hebrews 12:1–8. Read also Hebrews 12:1–7; Philippians 3:13–14).

Is there a high calling? You can settle for just being a

Christian, but I am not settling, because I know there is more. Until I awake in His likeness, I will not be satisfied.

> *Therefore leaving the principles of the doctrine of Christ, let us go on unto perfection; not laying again the foundation of repentance from dead works, and of faith toward God* (Hebrews 6:1. Read Hebrews 6:1–8).

This is why a backslider has difficulty with being restored. If we have gone through deliverance, know the power of God is there to set us free and we walk away, then there are no more answers for us. God can keep us from failing His grace. His Church is going to go out with power and life.

> *And we know that all things work together for good to them that love God, to them who are the called according to his purpose* (Romans 8:28. Read Romans 8:28–37).

We are more than conquerors and can accomplish so much for Jesus Christ. We can surpass the maintenance of our deliverance and do great exploits for Jesus. We have vast opportunities in the Church today, yet we still fool around. God doesn't force anything on us; He shows us His Word. He's given us His life. He's given us all the tools to fight. It is up to us. The devil himself forces an entrance. God is different—if we do not open our hearts, He will not come in. We are royalty. He is able to keep us from falling, from sinning, from going back to where we came from.

Through the power of His Blood, we not only maintain our deliverance, but we are changed from glory to glory. As His character increases in our lives and our "old man" decreases, we can walk perfect and blameless before Him and do great exploits.

This is an abridged version of this message.
Please contact us to order the tape of
this entire message.

Chapter 10

The Glory

The Lord spoke to me about the glory, and I believe God is going to bring us forth as He deals with our hearts. Then, just as God promised, His glory has to come. We have to come forth in that which God is going to do. This is about God building His Church and coming forth in His Body. We are the Church of the living God.

I want to say the glory is not a halo, or a cloud or a physical presence. I looked up references to John 2 in the dictionary. I'm just going to bring that word out and I'm going to tell you what the word *glory* means.

> *This beginning of miracles did Jesus in Caana of Galilee, and manifested forth his glory; and his disciples believed on him* (John 2:11).

This is the first miracle Jesus did—the turning of water into wine. This was the first manifestation of His glory, and His disciples believed on Him. What is it going to take for people to come back to the Church? The glory. What is the glory? Miracles, as described here in this reference. The miracles must come back to the Church, and this should be our goal. God is going to bring the miracles back, as it says in John 2, because they are "manifested for His glory."

The word *glory* means dignity, honour, praise and worship. People will learn to worship God when they see signs. In His Name, we shall cast out devils, we shall speak with new tongues. The Gospel of Mark speaks about it. But I believe there is a deficiency in the Church, and when I say "The Church," all of us are incorporated. We can all agree that there has to be more of Him and His power available to us today. In Jesus' day, where there was unbelief, He did no miracles. And there is still unbelief today; as a result, there will be no miracles now. People have to believe in their own hearts.

Do you think that we need the glory? Do you think that the glory is going to come back to the Church? As the devil manifests in the world system, so God is going to manifest Himself in His Church. The devil is not greater than God; God is the greater power. He created the devil for His own divine purposes, so it is not possible for the created to be greater than the Creator.

Let's turn to Romans 3:20-28:

Therefore by the deeds of the law there shall no flesh be justified in his sight: for by the law is the knowledge of sin. But now the righteousness of God without the law is manifested, being witnessed by the law and the prophets; Even the righteousness of God which is by faith of Jesus Christ unto all and upon all them that believe: for there is no difference: For all have sinned, and come short of the glory of God; Being justified freely by his grace through the redemption that is in

Christ Jesus: whom God hath sent forth to be a propitiation through faith in his blood, to declare his righteousness for the remission of sins that are past, through the forbearance of God; to declare, I say, at this time his righteousness: that he might be just, and the justifier of him which believeth in Jesus. Where is boasting then? It is exluded. By what law? of works? Nay: but by the law of faith. Therefore we conclude that a man is justified by faith without the deeds of the law.

As God sets us free, through the ministry of deliverance, the world out there will see that something about us has changed and is different from them. When the joy of the Lord is operating in full force, in and through our lives, we are going to see many people coming to us to know how to be saved. Now is the time, even when we see the unrest—this is the time when the world is looking for an answer. The Church has the answer and has the only reality. We, as the Church, have the answer: it is in the Word of God and it is in us.

If the light in us is dim, how can we effectively dispel the darkness? The world is in darkness, but as soon as we come in, we should bring light into each room, each situation. We cannot even tell that many Christians *are* Christian—our fallen countenances are sullen, and we wear the world on our shoulders. You know what? I had to learn to practice to smile and change my countenance. I looked in the mirror and I said, "Wow, is that how I look?" Our countenances have to change. Many do not even know how to smile. How can we draw someone to Christ if our face tells anyone looking at us to get away? We should not even have to tell people about Jesus—they should see our Christianity on our faces. Right away, as we walk into a room, the face presents itself.

Sin has marred the glory in our faces and in our lives. We cannot be smiling when we have hidden sins in our hearts. We do not really need any discernment to look at some people's faces and know they have problems. Now, what kind of facial expressions are we giving off—what kind of glory are we giving off? God can restore our joy and our countenances through the power of deliverance. Sin has hindered God's plan for His glory to be seen in His people. *"For all have sinned, and come short of the glory of God"* (Romans 3:23). So, all have sinned and come short of the glory of God.

Let me just go to Haggai 2:8–9, Old Testament Scriptures. Verse 8: *"The silver is mine, and the gold is mine, saith the Lord of hosts."* You see, when our lives shine out the life of Jesus Christ, it is glorifying to the Lord. When He calls us by His Name, we need to represent Him well. We cannot be just "Church Christians"—we must be Christian in our homes, in our workplace, the shopping centre and in our cars. One true test is in our homes. If you want to know what a true Christian you are, consider how you behave with your family after you leave the church. The Lord can and will show us what is in our hearts; after He shows us, He wants to remove those things in our hearts that are not glorifying to Him, so that we can be as pure gold. In this He will be glorified. And because of our sin, we have come short of anything worthy for Him to be glorified.

Many people are dying out there. There are many people looking for answers now. But the world will only wake up to the right answers when the Church wakes up, and recognizes her place. Now, verse 9 of Haggai 2:

The glory of this latter house shall be greater than of the former, saith the Lord of hosts: and in this place will I give peace, saith the Lord of hosts."

Let's just turn to Joel 2, quickly, because I can't read this Scripture without reading Joel 2:23.

Be glad then, ye children of Zion, and rejoice in the Lord your God: for he hath given you the former rain moderately, and he will cause to come down for you the rain, the former rain, and the latter rain in the first month.

When the Scriptures say, "Be glad," we should be! We should not wear our pain on our faces. I am not saying anything that I have not experienced myself; I know there are times when I have a headache and my head feels as though it is going to split open, and someone will call me for prayer. After I have prayed for them, I am free from my headache, completely healed.

Church, it's going to cost you something. How do we expect to get something from God without putting something in? God is not Santa Claus; He is going to call the Church to order. We need to know that God has put His Spirit in us not that we should be weak, but that we should be strong. What causes us to be strong is getting on our knees and praying that God will strengthen us. In the name of Jesus, I want us to stand as servants of God, with His complete possession of our lives. We need to be determined not to play Church.

Where are we going to find ourselves when sorrows increase? The Church is still not praying and the Church is still not serious. What is it going to take for the Church to be awakened? We need to be awakened, Church, because God wants to restore His glory to His Church. And it will be you and me who accomplish this work. Jesus Christ is not going to come back to do the work; He finished His work in the earth. The work has to be finished with this latter-day Church. Continuing with Joel 2:24–25,

And the floors shall be full of wheat, and the vats shall overflow with wine and oil. And I will restore to you the years that the locust hath eaten, the cankerworm, and the caterpillar, and the palmerworm, my great army which I sent among you.

Jesus Christ has come to break every generational curse from your life. Stand up, Church, and be accounted for God.

In whom we have redemption through his blood, even the forgiveness of sins: Who is the image of the invisible God, the firstborn of every creature (Colossians 1:14–15).

We have the best. There is nothing more out there in the world's system. We have the best; there is nothing better than this gospel. He is our pattern Son. He shows us the way. He bought us. He died. He took on our sicknesses and our diseases. We have to lay them down and give them to Him. That's why He came.

For by him were all things created, that are in heaven, and that are in earth, visible and invisible, whether they be thrones, or dominions, or principalities, or powers: all things were created by him and for him (Colossians 1:16).

Even the trials you go through are created for His purpose, so you can come forth.

And he is before all things, and by him all things consist. And he is the head of the body, the church: who is the beginning, the firstborn from the dead; that in all things he might have

the preeminence. For it pleased the Father that in him should all fulness dwell; And, having made peace through the blood of his cross, by him to reconcile all things unto himself; by him, I say, whether they be things in earth, or things in heaven (Colossians 1:17–20).

One night I went to my bed and dreamt about a monster. And the word I heard in my dream was *monstrosorous*. We do not understand that there are greater judgments coming on our land; some churches think we will be gone somewhere, but where are we going with the baggage of wickedness in our hearts? We need to get rid of those things from our hearts. We are not going anywhere until God cleans up His Church. He is coming back for a Church without spot or wrinkle. You are going to be here with all of us, taking responsibility for your heart.

If ye continue in the faith grounded and settled, and be not moved away from the hope of the gospel, which ye have heard, and which was preached to every creature which is under heaven; whereof I Paul am made a minister; Who now rejoice in my sufferings for you, and fill up that which is behind of the afflictions of Christ in my flesh for his body's sake, which is the church (Colossians 1:23–24).

You need to read that over and over again. Paul was a man just like us; he persecuted the Church and God woke him up out of that stupor. Then he was totally sold out. This is what it is going to take, Church. If you are not sold out to God, you are going to be left behind.

Whereof I am made a minister, according to the dispensation of God which is given to me for you, to fulfil the word of God; Even the mystery which hath been hid from ages and from generations, but now is made manifest to his saints: To whom God would make known what is the riches of the glory of this mystery among the Gentiles; which is Christ in you, the hope of glory (Colossians 1:25-27).

There is a reason why Christ is in us. We are not just going to be saved and be happy. Some of us just jump up in the house of God and when the dance is over, we go back to our routine. We need to change.

Whom we preach, warning every man, and teaching every man in all wisdom; that we may present every man perfect in Christ teaching every man in all wisdom; that we may present every man perfect in Christ Jesus (Colossians 1:28).

If I did not warn you, blood would be on my hands. I have one responsibility, and that is to lay the foundation of the Word of God. Then it is up to each and every individual who hears (or reads). He is the only One through whom we can be perfected. We cannot be perfected by doctrine or religion, only through the power of Jesus Christ. This is why He came.

"*Whereunto I also labour, striving according to his working, which worketh in me mightily*" (Colossians 1:29). What will awaken us to realize that we must labour and strive? We are lazy and the Church is asleep. What is it going to take to wake us up?

Cease not to give thanks for you, making mention of you in my prayers; That the God of our Lord Jesus Christ, the Father of glory, may give unto you the spirit of wisdom and revelation in the knowledge of him: The eyes of your understanding being enlightened; that ye may know what is the hope of his calling, and what the riches of the glory of his inheritance in the saints, Which he wrought in Christ, when he raised him from the dead, and set him at his own right hand in the heavenly places, Far above all principality, and power, and might, and dominion, and every name that is named, not only in this world, but also in that which is to come: And hath put all things under his feet, and gave him to be the head over all things to the church, Which is his body, the fulness of him that filleth all in all (Ephesians 1:16–23).

If you do not know the hope of His calling for your life, you are going to miss His plan and His Kingdom. The hope of His calling is not just going to church, although it is a part of it. We have to measure up to the Word of God, not according to what I think or what sister so-and-so thinks, but to this Word that "filleth all in all."

When the new millennium came in, everybody was prepared. Some bought food and water—even kerosene lamps sold out. We were on our guard, and I knew that nothing was going to happen, because everybody was watching. The Word of God tells us the opposite: He will come at a time when we do not expect Him. We listen to the media, and that media will poison us. Many in the Church believe the media, but the Bible should be your report—read it well. We need to persuade men and women. God wants men and women with strong backbones.

We must show the world we are different, and let the glory come back to the Church where it belongs. Too long have the hospitals been filled. The Church is filled with sickness and disease, and we need to see changes with healing coming back to the Church. It is time that we got on our knees. This is what it is going to take, Church.

The Bible speaks about a remnant. We have religion. A

lot of us even have Pentecost and are still religious. God wants to knock out our religion. We do everything that looks right, but is our heart right with God? You see, God sees every little detail of our hearts and we cannot fool Him. A year ago, the Lord showed me that God was going to bring judgment. This society has been so perverted and so bold. God destroyed Sodom; only Lot and his two daughters were saved. Let us not be like Lot, contented to be in the plains and doing nothing. We see the wrong and we are vexed for a moment, but then we move away. We are not crying at the altar. We need to come forth, Church! The Church does not want to be disciplined, but if you are not disciplined, you are a bastard. You are not a son—you are not going to come into maturity. You will not come into the fullness of the glory God has for you.

This is an abridged version of this message.
Please contact us to order the tape of
this entire message.

Epilogue

My prayer is that these messages and testimonies have been a blessing to you and have opened the door for you to be set free, healed and restored by the power of the Holy Ghost. Today, my husband and I pastor a church called Mount Zion House of Praise. God has us lead missionary teams to various countries and continues to use us to minister deliverance to the Church worldwide.

We are devoted by God's grace to seeing others healed, leaving family behind many times to minister to the needs of others. As the Lord spoke to me years ago, "You take care of My business and I'll take care of yours." My husband and I have raised three very beautiful children, all serving the Lord, all upstanding Christians with a tremendous heritage.

If anything within this book has challenged you, we encourage you to get in touch with us. We know that Jesus Christ has come to redeem a people and He will return to marry a perfect bride. We pray that we will all come into the unity of that faith, and that we will all be partakers with that great company of saints.

We can be contacted at:
Mount Zion House of Praise
P.O. Box 51033,
Unit 379, 25 Peel Centre Drive,
Brampton, Ontario, CANADA L6T 5M2